CHURCH AND NAT
LECTU

BY

William Temple

CHURCH AND NATION: THE BISHOP PADDOCK LECTURES FOR 1914-15

Published by Scriptura Press

New York City, NY

First published circa 2016

Copyright © Scriptura Press, 2015

All rights reserved

ABOUT SCRIPTURA PRESS

<u>Scriptura Press</u> is a Christian company that makes Christian works available and affordable to all. We are a non-denominational publishing group that shares the teachings of the Scripture, whether in the form of sermons or histories of the Church.

PREFACE

When I received and accepted the invitation to deliver the Paddock Lectures for the season 1914-1915, no one imagined that these years were destined to have the historical significance which they must now possess for all time. I was myself one of those who had allowed concern for social reform, and internal problems generally, to occupy my mind almost to the exclusion of foreign questions. I was prepared to stake a good deal upon what seemed to me the improbability of any outbreak of European war. For all who took this view the events of recent months have involved perhaps a greater re-shaping of fundamental notions than was required by people who had thought probable such a catastrophe as that in which we are now involved. I found it impossible to concentrate my mind upon any subject wholly unconnected with the war, while at the same time it would have been in the last degree unsuitable that in my lectures to American Theological Students I should deliver myself of such views as I had formed concerning the rights and wrongs of the war itself, or the questions at stake in it.

These lectures, therefore, represent an attempt to think out afresh the underlying problems which for a Christian are fundamental in regard not only to this war but to war in general—the place of Nationality in the scheme of Divine Providence and the duty of the Church in regard to the growth of nations.

But in a preface it may be permissible to say what would be inappropriate in the Lectures themselves, and first I would take this opportunity of reiterating certain convictions which have formed the basis of a series of pamphlets issued under the auspices of a Committee drawn from various Christian bodies and political parties, of which I have had the honour to be Editor:

1. That Great Britain was in August morally bound to declare war and is no less bound to carry the war to a decisive issue;

2. That the war is none the less an outcome and a revelation of the un-Christian principles which have dominated the life of Western Christendom and of which both the Church and the nations have need to repent;

3. That followers of Christ, as members of the Church, are linked to one another in a fellowship which transcends all divisions of nationality or race;

4. That the Christian duties of love and forgiveness are as binding in time of war as in time of peace;

5. That Christians are bound to recognise the insufficiency of mere compulsion for overcoming evil, and to place supreme reliance upon spiritual forces and in particular upon the power and method of the Cross;

6. That only in proportion as Christian principles dictate the terms of settlement will a real and lasting peace be secured;

7. That it is the duty of the Church to make an altogether new effort to realise and apply to all the relations of life its own positive ideal of brotherhood and fellowship;

1: That with God all things are possible.

These propositions were very carefully drafted by the Committee referred to above and entirely represent my own beliefs; but there is something more which I would add. The new Triple Alliance of Germany, Austria, and Turkey is no accident; it is the combination of just those three Powers which openly and avowedly believe in oppression—that is, in the imposition by force of the standards accepted by one race upon people of another race. All nations have at one time or another practised oppression; certainly Great Britain is not free from the charge, and the history of Russia has many dark pages in this respect. But we can all claim that when we have been guilty of oppression it has been under the influence of fear, whether of revolution, anarchism, or some other force thought to be disruptive of the State. With our enemies this is not so. We all know about Turkey; it is the essentially Mohammedan power, and Mohammedanism is the religion of oppression; it believes in imposing its faith by means of the sword. The Austrian Empire consists of three divisions in each of which one race is imposing its manner of life upon another. In Austria-proper the Germans oppress the Czechs; in Galicia the Poles have, in some degree at least, oppressed the Ruthenes; in Hungary the Magyars have systematically and avowedly oppressed the Roumanians in the east, and the Croats in the south and west. Germany has shown her political faith by her conduct in Alsace-Lorraine, and still more in Poland. Nothing has yet appeared so illuminating with regard to what is at stake in this war, as Prince Bülow's chapter on Poland in his book, Imperial Germany; he describes what seems to us the most grinding oppression with obvious self-contentment and without a question of its righteousness; and there have been abundant signs that, at least, many people in Germany are willing to impose German Kultur by the sword as Mohammedans impose belief in their prophet.

If this is true, and if the analysis in my lectures of the Christian function of the State and of the principles of the Kingdom of God is sound, then it becomes clear that this war is being fought to determine whether in the next period the Christian or the directly anti-Christian method shall have an increase of influence. The three most democratic of the great Western Powers—Great Britain, France, and Italy—in conjunction with Russia, which is after all profoundly democratic in its local life though imperially it is a military autocracy, are linked together in a natural union on behalf of freedom as they understand it, against an idea embodied and embattled which is in exact opposition to all they live for. It was therefore no surprise to find that all the citizens of the United States with whom I came in contact were quite definitely upon the side of the Allies in sympathy. To advocate war in the name of Christ is to adopt a position which looks self-contradictory and which certainly involves immense responsibility, and yet if our people can maintain the attitude of mind in which they entered on the war and can secure at the end a settlement harmonious with that frame of mind, I believe they will have served the Kingdom of God through fighting, better than it was possible to do at this moment in human history by any other means.

W.T.

Lecture II. in this series is almost identical with the pamphlet Our Need of a Catholic Church—No. 19 of Papers for War Time. In Lectures I. and III. I am under great obligation to Professor A. G. Hogg, though my position is not at all identical with his.

LECTURE I

CHURCH AND NATION
LECTURE I
THE KINGDOM OF FREEDOM

"And Jesus, full of the Holy Spirit, returned from the Jordan, and was led by the Spirit in the wilderness during forty days, being tempted of the Devil."—S. Luke iv. 1.

Our Lord, in accepting for Himself the title of the Messiah, or the Christ, claimed that it was His function to inaugurate upon earth the Kingdom of God. Whatever else might at that time be believed about the Messiah, this at least was universally held, that the Messiah, when He came, would inaugurate upon earth the Kingdom of God. That is the task of the Lord's ministry; that is the task to which we, as His followers, are pledged; and at this time when the civilisation, which for nearly two thousand years has been under the Christian influence, has culminated in as great a catastrophe as has ever beset any civilisation, Christian or Pagan, it is well for us to go back and ask, What are the fundamental principles of the Kingdom which Christ founded, what the method by which He founded it, and what are the principles and methods which He rejected?

There were various anticipations of the way in which the promised Christ would do His work; but broadly speaking there were two main types of expectation. There were those who supposed that the Messiah when He came, would rule in the manner of an earthly ruler, establishing righteousness by the ordinary methods of law and political authority, and this expectation undoubtedly derived some colour from the way in which Isaiah had envisaged the coming Christ:[#]

[#] Isaiah ix, 6, 7.

It is a king ruling upon the throne of David that is suggested; and while it is only the most foolish literalism which will say that the Prophet himself was committed to such a view, it was natural enough for those who read his writings to conceive of the Messiah as acting after that fashion.

The people went into captivity; and when they returned, it was not to any realised Kingdom of God upon earth, but rather to difficulties greater than had ever confronted them before, until at last Antiochus Epiphanes initiated the great persecution whose aim was to stamp out altogether the worship of Jehovah, setting up as he did in the very Temple Court at Jerusalem the altar of Zeus, on which swine were sacrificed—"the abomination of desolation standing where it ought not." Out of the fiery furnace of that persecution comes the glowing prophecy of Daniel. What is the answer which he conceives God as giving to the blasphemer Antiochus? It is nothing less than the divine judgment and the mission of the divine Deliverer:[#]

[#] Daniel vii, 9, 10, 13, 14.

This conception of the Messiah, coming in the clouds of Heaven, establishing the Kingdom of God by so manifest an exhibition of the divine authority with which He is endowed, that all doubt and hesitation are quite impossible, is that which took the greatest hold upon the religious imagination of Israel, and particularly of that great body of people, the heirs of the tradition of the Maccabees, inheritors of the heroism which had stood out against the persecution, whom we know as the sect of the Pharisees—men who lived in the strength of a fellowship that had behind it the greatest religious tradition in all the world, but who, because they trusted more to their tradition than to the God who inspired it, were unable to recognise the still further call of God when it came to them. The literature of the period between the Old and the New Testament shows how wide and deep was the influence of Daniel's vision upon their Messianic hopes.

At His baptism, the Lord is called to begin His Messianic work; the voice which He heard from Heaven spoke words which were by all interpreters of the time believed to refer to the Messiah:—"Thou art my beloved son; in thee I am well pleased." The Messiah will be endowed with Divine authority and power. How shall He use it? And immediately the Lord goes into the wilderness to face the temptations that arose from precisely the conviction that His Messianic work is even now to begin.

The temptation has two sides to it—an inward and an outward. As regards Himself, what does the temptation mean? Let us remind ourselves that there was apparently no one with Him in this crisis; the story, as we have it, must come from Himself. It is His own account (of course in parable form, like so much else in His teaching) of the struggle of those early days. What is meant by the parable concerning the turning of stones into bread? Surely for Himself it is the temptation to use the power, with which us the Christ of Cod He is endowed, for the satisfaction of His own needs, and that in such a way as will do no kind of harm to anybody else. No one will be the worse for his satisfying His hunger in that way. It is a self-concern from which nobody can suffer; it is perfectly innocent and perfectly rational. But no! It is not for any selfish purpose, however harmless, that the power of God is given; selfishness in its most innocent form is set aside.

How shall He set about His work? Shall He fulfil that expectation which Isaiah's vision had fostered? He looks out on the kingdoms of the earth and the glory of them, and He knows that they can be His, if He will fall down and worship the Prince of the power of this world. Shall He use worldly methods to convert the world to God? No; worldliness in its most attractive form is set aside.

Or shall He fulfil the expectation encouraged by the vision of the Son of Man in Daniel, appearing with the clouds of Heaven, descending upon Jerusalem up-borne by angels, giving that sign from Heaven which the Pharisees, who particularly adopted this view of the Messiah, were afterwards going to demand so frequently? From His answer we know that this is a temptation not only to give them a sign, but to secure it for Himself, for the answer is "Thou shalt not tempt,"—that is, Thou shalt not put to the proof—"the Lord thy God." The promise of God is to be trusted, not tested. The test comes as we obey the command and in that sense every act of faith is an experiment, but there must be no test cases to see whether God fulfils His promise. Infidelity in its most insidious form is set aside.

But there is an outward aspect also to the temptations. Shall He use His power to satisfy the bodily needs of men? Shall He exert a power parallel with that of political rulers, which will coerce their conduct without first winning their free allegiance? Shall He give such proof of divine authority that any doubt, intellectual or otherwise, becomes impossible? No; not any of these. And as He leaves the temptation vanquished, what He has set aside is precisely every method of controlling men's action without winning their hearts and wills. He has rejected coercion; He has decided to appeal to Freedom.

What is left? At first, only the commission to proclaim the Kingdom; and He comes proclaiming it. All through the early part of the ministry He moves from place to place preaching or proclaiming the Kingdom of God. He does not at present announce that He is King of that Kingdom; it is the Kingdom itself on which all attention is concentrated. He has indeed the power to do works of mercy, and when with that power He stands in the face of human need, He must for very love exert the power and satisfy the need; so people come crowding around Him, attracted by His wonder-working. But that is not what He desires. The disciples are excited about it; but He has gone out a long while before dawn, and is alone in prayer; and when St. Peter finds Him, and says "All men are seeking Thee," He does not say, "Then let us go to them," but, on the contrary, "Let us go into the villages that I may preach—that I may make my proclamation—there also."[#] As the deadness, the indifference, and hostility of the people gradually shows itself to be invincible, He gathers about Him those whose hearts have been touched, and from among them chooses twelve, "that they may be with Him."[#] They are to live in His company, catching His Spirit, learning to understand Him. With them He goes on two long journeys—north-west to Tyre and Sidon, and then north-east, to Caesarea Philippi; through all those journeys they are alone with their Master, moving through country outside the boundaries of the Jewish religion, and therefore free from controversy.

[#] S. Mark i, 35-38.

[#] S. MArk iii, 14.

At Caesarea Philippi He feels that the time is ripe, and asks them, "Who do men say that I am?" They mention the various conjectures ... Elijah; John the Baptist; one of the Prophets. "Who say ye that I am?" And St. Peter with a leap of inspired insight answers: "Thou art the Messiah."[#]

[#] S. Mark viii, 27-30.

The Lord recognises that this is the revelation of God to faith: "Blessed art thou, Simon, Son of Jonah; flesh and blood hath not revealed it unto thee, but my Father which is in heaven."[#] Immediately that He has been thus spontaneously recognised, He begins to say what He had never said before: "The Son of Man must suffer." The Son of Man is the title of the Messiah in glory, as He was conceived in Daniel's vision and the Apocalyptic writings which drew their inspiration from it. "The Son of Man must suffer;" that is the great Messianic act; that is the way in which the Kingdom of God shall be founded. But it was not what St. Peter meant. "Peter took Him, and began to rebuke Him ... Be it far from Thee, Lord; this shall not be unto Thee." And our Lord recognises the voice of the tempter in the wilderness, who bade Him take thought for self.... "Get thee behind me, Satan, for thou thinkest not God's thoughts, but men's thoughts."[#]

[#] S. Matthew xvi, 17.

[#] S. Matthew xvi, 22, 23.

Just as, when once He was spontaneously recognised, He began to set forth the new conception of the Messiahship, "The Son of Man must suffer;" so too He immediately starts on that last journey to Jerusalem which culminates with the Cross. Arrived at Jerusalem, He arranges the triumphal entry. He carefully fulfils Zechariah's prophecy—thus claiming the Messiahship, and challenging the religious rulers. But the prophecy which He thus selects for deliberate fulfilment is one which represents the Messiah as a civil, not a military authority (for this is the meaning of the ass as distinguished from the horse), and as one who shall speak Peace to the nations.[#] It is the conception of the Messiah which in all the Old Testament has least suggestion of coercion and is therefore the nearest to His own.

[#] Zechariah ix, 9, 10.

But the primary purpose of the triumphal entry is no doubt to make His claim and issue His challenge. On the journey and after the entry itself He declares with increasing emphasis that the Kingdom of God is at hand; those who stood there should see it come with power; and as He stands before Caiaphas, He answers the question "Art Thou the Christ? with the words, I am, and from this time[#] there shall be the Son of Man seated on the right hand of power." Daniel's prophecy is here and now fulfilled. In the moment that love completes its sacrifice in death, the glory of God is fully made known and the power of His Kingdom is come; this is the Lord's own Apocalypse.[#]

[#] Different words in St. Matthew and St. Luke, but agreeing in sense, which sense the authorised version spoils.

[#] See .: The Apocalyptic Consciousness.

So He had spoken on that last journey. "Ye know that they which are accounted to rule over the Gentiles lord it over them, and their great ones exercise authority over them. But it is not so among you; but whosoever would become great among you shall be your minister, and whosoever shall be first among you shall be servant of all, for verily the Son of Man came"— (again the title of the Messiah in Glory)—"not to be ministered unto, but to minister; and to give His life a ransom for many."[#]

[#] S. Mark x, 42-45.

So, too, St. John records His saying that in precisely this way he would win His royalty—"I, if I be lifted up from the earth, will draw all men unto me."[#] The Cross was foreseen by the Lord to be what, as we look back, we know that it has been—the throne of His glory and His power; and the capacity to realise it as such is for St. Paul the touchstone of character, the test of election—"We preach a Messiah on a Cross—to Jews a scandal and to Gentiles an absurdity, but to the very people who are called, whether Jews or Greeks, a Messiah who is God's power and God's wisdom."[#]

[#] S. John xii, 32.

[#] 1 Cor. i, 23, 24.

Here then is the mode of God's power, and we know that it can be no other; for if God is truly King, He must be King of our hearts and wills, and not only of our conduct. There is only one way to win men's hearts and wills, that is by showing love; and there is only one way to show love, and that is by sacrifice, by doing or suffering what, apart from our love, we should not choose to do or suffer. Sacrifice is the Divine activity; Calvary is the mode of the Divine omnipotence. It is the actual Divine method and the ideal human method.

As we come to consider how far it has become also the actual human method, we are confronted at the outset by the sheer impossibility of our applying this method, just because we have not in ourselves the necessary love.

Our perfection, we are told, is to consist in just that quality which shows the Father's perfection, namely, that He is kind to the unthankful and evil, and makes His sun to rise on the evil and good and sends His rain on the just and on the unjust; and we are to be perfect in the way that He is perfect.[#]

[#] S. Matthew v, 43-48.

But until we reach that perfection we cannot imitate His action; for a man's act is not what He intends; nor is it the mere motion of his body; but it is the whole train of circumstances that he initiates. Christ in His perfect purity may stand before the woman taken in her sin and say, "Neither do I condemn thee," because there is no possibility that she will interpret His mercy as condonation of the sin; but if we said it, people would so interpret it, and usually quite rightly so.

Our problem then is so to guide our conduct that we come as near as we are capable of coming to the divine ideal that is set forth in Christ, and that we come perpetually closer and closer to it.

The Lord in His temptation rejected all use of force and substituted for it the appeal of love expressed in sacrifice, so far as the actual and positive building of His Kingdom is concerned. For us there must always be some use of the lower method, because we are incapable of applying the highest. If any man, when he is confronted with evil which he can prevent by the exercise of force, refrains from doing it, we must immediately put to him the question, "But did you so suffer under that act of evil that there is any hope of your suffering proving to be the redemption of the evil-doer? If so, well and good; but, if not, then you are idle and cowardly, not Christian." No one who is not a Christian in spirit can perform the Christian act; and the Sermon on the Mount is not a code of rules to be mechanically followed; it is the description of the life which any man will spontaneously lead when once the Spirit of Christ has taken complete possession of his heart.

And yet there is a perfectly legitimate use of force also, and a use which our Lord Himself makes of it. We may use force in various circumstances in spite of the fact that for the positive work of the building His Kingdom the Lord rejected it. It is legitimate, in the first place, when it is applied to immature characters—characters which are, as all our characters are in early childhood, a chaos of impulses and instincts, as yet unregulated by any governing principle. Here it may be necessary simply to restrain the activity of one set of impulses without converting the heart or will of the person to whom that restraint is applied, merely in order to give the other side of nature its chance of development. So in education it is legitimate to employ force in this restraining way for the sake of the development which is made possible thereby in the other parts of nature.

But our Lord's example also shows us that the use of force is permissible in dealing with those who are so case-hardened that the appeal of love can never reach them until their present state of mind is broken up. It is sometimes said that the Lord never made use of physical force; but whether or not that is true[#]—the question is unimportant, because for all moral purposes there is no difference whatever between physical and non-physical force. The appeal to force always means the appeal to pain or inconvenience, for these are the only things that force can inflict upon one. Physical force may break a man's bones; but one may enforce a certain kind of conduct by the threat, for example, of social ostracism, which might break his heart; and there is no difference whatever between the two, except that the second is a more refined form of cruelty. Now in our Lord's denunciation of the Pharisees, in those words which are thrown, burning and smashing, into the self-complacent contentment of those upholders of tradition, there is every moral quality of force and violence. Their aim is to batter down a state of mind, the state of mind which cannot receive the appeal of love, as it shows when it stands beneath the very Cross and only jeers. But this use of force is only negative and preparatory; it is the effort of love to make ready for the rebuilding which only love's own method can really accomplish. Only with characters quite immature and liable to develop in many different directions, can force be used, except in this wholly preparatory way; and even there its work is preparatory, for at that stage everything that is done is still preparatory.

[#] e.g., whether or not He employed the scourge of small cords to drive men from the Temple Courts as He certainly did the animals; the Greek words suggest that He did not.

It is sometimes said that society rests upon force. Of course it does not, and it could not, because force is a dead thing which can only operate as human wills direct it; and, however much force there may be in the maintenance of society, that force itself must be controlled by the consent of human wills. It is true, however, that society, as we know it, rests simultaneously upon two contradictory principles, upon the principle of antagonism and the principle of fellowship. So far as it is represented by the police force, it rests upon antagonism. Men are selfish; in their selfishness they are brought into conflict with one another. In order that anyone may be able to enjoy, however selfishly, any property or comfort in life, it is necessary to restrain to some degree the selfishness of all the rest; and to secure that restraint placed upon others, a man submits to a similar restraint upon himself. And so we arrive at that contract of which Plato speaks: "the contract neither to commit nor to suffer injury."[#] But, at the same time, as Plato immediately afterwards points out, society would arise quite equally if men were wholly altruistic, because men's natures are different, and they need one another for support, for protection, and for the very instinct of fellowship.[#] Now those principles are both present in all actual societies; and progress has consisted of the steady development of the principle of co-operation and fellowship, at the expense of the principle of competition and antagonism.

[#] [Greek: méte adikeîn méte adikîsthai.] Republic ii. 359*a*.

[#] The whole Ideal State. Republic ii, 369*b* to vii end.

That has been what we have meant in the last resort by political progress; but the conclusion inevitably follows that society makes progress precisely in that degree in which it realises more and more a relationship of love between its various members, and becomes the Kingdom which Christ came on earth to found. Thus, at the very outset of our enquiry we find that the principles of secular progress and of the Divine revelation in Christ are identical.

I shall venture in a subsequent lecture to trace out the way in which, as I think, further progress in accordance with this principle will lead us.

But let me close this lecture by recalling our thoughts to that ideal method for men, which is the actual method of God, setting this in the words of a fable which I take from the masterpiece of the most Russian of the Russian novelists—Dostoievsky—merely throwing it into my own language.

In the days of the Inquisition, this fable runs, our Lord returned to earth, and visited a city where it was at work. As He moved about, men forgot their cares and sorrows. He healed the sick folk as of old, and meeting with a funeral procession where a mother was mourning the loss of her only son, He stopped the procession, and restored the dead boy to life.

That was in the Cathedral Square, and at that moment there came out from the Cathedral doors the Grand Inquisitor, an old man over ninety years of age, clad now, not in the Cardinal's robe in which only the day before he had condemned a score of heretics to the stake, but in a simple cassock, with only two guards in attendance. Seeing what was done he turned to the guards and said, "Arrest Him." They moved forward to obey; and he sent the Prisoner to a cell in the dungeon.

That night the Grand Inquisitor visited his Prisoner, and to all that he said the Prisoner made no reply. "I know why Thou art come," said the Inquisitor; "Thou art come to spoil our work, to repeat Thy great mistake in the wilderness, and to give men again Thy fatal gift of freedom. What did the great wise spirit offer Thee there? Just the three things by which men may be controlled—bread and authority and mystery. He bade Thee take bread as the instrument of Thy work; men will follow one who gives them bread. But Thou wouldest not; men were to follow Thee out of love and devotion or not at all. We have had to correct Thy work, or there would be few to follow Thee. He bade Thee assume authority; men will obey one who gives commands, and punishes the disobedient. But Thou wouldest not; men were to obey out of love and devotion or not at all. We have had to correct Thy work, or there would be few to obey Thee. He bade Thee show some marvel that men might be persuaded and believe. But Thou wouldest not; men were to believe from perception of Thy grace and truth or not at all. We have had to correct Thy work and hedge Thee about with mystery, or there would be few to believe. And which of us has served mankind the better? Thy appeal was to the few strong souls. We have cared for the weak. Many who would be disorderly and miserable have been made orderly and happy. And now Thou art come to spoil our work and repeat Thy great mistake in the wilderness by giving to men again Thy fatal gift of freedom, through trust in the power of love. But it shall not be; for to-morrow I shall burn Thee."

The Grand Inquisitor ceased; and still the Prisoner made no reply; but He rose from where He sat, and crossed the cell, and kissed the old man on his bloodless lips. Then the Inquisitor too, rose, and opened the door; "Go," he said. The Prisoner passed out into the night and was not seen again.

And the old man? That kiss burns in his heart. But he has not altered his opinion or his practice.

LECTURE II

CHURCH AND STATE

"He put all things in subjection under his feet, and gave him to be head over all things to the Church, which is his body, the fulness of him that, all in all, is being fulfilled."—Ephesians i, 22, 23.

If one of the great saints of the early Church had been told that in the year 1915 the world would still be waiting for the final consummation, and had tried to conceive the life of men and nations as it would be after that long period of Christian influence, what would his conception have been? Surely he would have expected that all nations would be linked together in the Holy Communion, the Fellowship of Saints. Roman, Spaniard, African, Syrian, those strange Germans, and the barbarous Britons who lived in the remotest corner of the earth, might have maintained their own varieties of culture, but each would find his joy and pride in offering his contribution to the life of the whole family of nations. Rooted in knowledge of the love of God, their life would grow luxuriantly and bear fruit in love of one another and service of the common cause. Inspiring each and knitting all together, the Holy Catholic Church, fulfilling itself in service of the world, would gather up all this exuberance of life and love into itself, and present it to the God and Father of mankind in unceasing adoration.

But the world in 1915 is not in the least like that. The old man of our selfish nature, selfish himself and therefore supposing that others must be selfish too, so that he relies upon the methods of cajolery and coercion, has indeed received the kiss of Christ; and while that kiss burns in his heart, so that sometimes he is roused to an aspiration after an order of things altogether different, his opinions and his conduct remain fundamentally unchanged. And the contrast between what is and what might have been is due in part, at least, to the failure of the Church to be true to its own commission. It is also because of this that no practical man dreams of turning to the Church to find the way out from the intolerable situation into which the nations have drifted.

An eminent politician is reported to have defined the Church on a recent occasion in the following terms: "The Church is, I suppose, a voluntary organisation for the maintenance of public worship in the interest of those who desire to join in it." And it is to be feared that many people regard it in some such way as that. But of course the Church is nothing of the kind; the

Church is the Body of Christ.

It is not a "voluntary organisation" any more than my body is a voluntary organisation either of limbs or of cells. No one could "voluntarily" join the Church, if by that were meant that the act originated in his own will. "No man can say Jesus is Lord, but in the Holy Spirit."[#] A man cannot make himself a Christian. The Apostles were made Christian by Christ Himself—"Ye did not choose Me, but I chose you"[#]; others were made Christian by the Apostles, or (as they always said) by Christ working in and through them; and so successive generations have been made Christian by the Spirit of Christ operative in the fellowship of His disciples—that is to say, in the Church. This is the aspect of truth expressed and preserved in the practice of infant baptism. We are Christians, if at all, not through any act initiated by our own will, but through our being received into the Christian fellowship and subjected to its influence. Just as we are born members of our family, so by our reception into the fellowship of the disciples we are "made members of Christ." In the one case as in the other, we may repudiate our membership or we may disgrace it; we can never abolish it. Let me hasten in parenthesis to add, that this is only one aspect of the truth, and the protest of those who object to infant baptism will be a valuable force in the Church, until we are finally secure against the temptation to regard a sacrament as a piece of magic. For of course it is true that, while no man can make himself a Christian by his own will, no man can be made a Christian against or without his will. It is precisely his will that the Spirit must lay hold of and convert, and the will can refuse conversion.

[#] 1 Cor. xii, 3

[#] S. John xv, 16.

The Church, then, is not a "voluntary organisation," but the creation of God in Christ. In fact it is the one immediate result of our Lord's earthly ministry. When His physical presence was withdrawn, there remained in the world, as fruit of His sojourn here, no volume of writings, no elaborated organisation with codified aims and methods, but a group of people who were united to one another because His Spirit lived and worked in each. And the great marvel lay in this: whereas all men realise that fellowship is better than rivalry, and yet fail to pass from one to the other because they are radically selfish both individually and corporately, in Christ men found themselves to be a real community in spite of their as yet unpurged selfishness. By the invasion of the Divine Life in Christ, the ideal itself, the life of fellowship, is given, and is made into the means of destroying just those qualities which had hitherto prevented its own realisation. The ecclesiastical organisations of to-day are not fellowships of this sort, but if the members of the Church lose their hold on this central principle of fellowship, as they have largely done, we are thrown back upon the futile effort to build up fellowship on the foundation of unredeemed selfishness.

As it is not true to say that the Church is a "voluntary" organisation, so also it is not true to say that it exists "for the maintenance of public worship," at least in the sense that most Englishmen would give to the words. Certainly the Church, consisting of men and women whom God of His sheer goodness has delivered from the power of darkness and translated into the kingdom of His dear Son, will find its first duty, as also its first impulse, in an abandonment of adoration. But if the God who is worshipped is not only some Jewish Jehovah or Mohammedan Allah, but the God and Father of our Lord Jesus Christ, this love and adoration of God will immediately express itself in the love and service of men, and especially in the passionate desire to share with others the supreme treasure of the knowledge of God. The Church, like its Master, will be chiefly concerned to seek and to save that which is lost, calling men everywhere to repent because the Kingdom of God is at hand. Worship is indeed the very breath of its life, but service of the world is the business of its life. It is the Body of Christ, that is to say, the instrument of His will, and His will is to save the world.

The spiritual life of men is not limited to this planet, and the fulfilment of the Church's task can never be here alone. The Church must call men from temporal to eternal hopes. But in this way it will do more than is possible in any other way to purify the temporal life itself. For most temporal goods are such that the more one person has the less there is for others, so that absorption in them leads inevitably to strife and war. But the eternal goods—love, joy, peace, loyalty, beauty, knowledge—are such that the fuller fruition of them by one leads of itself to fuller fruition by others also, and absorption in them leads without fail to brotherhood and fellowship.

It is not of worship, the breath of the church's life, but of service, the business of its life, that I wish to speak. But this can only be misleading if the other has not first been given prominence. The Church serves because it first worships. Only because it has in itself a foretaste of eternal life, the realised Kingdom of God, can it prepare the way of the Lord, so that His Kingdom may come on earth as it is in heaven.

One question which demands attention concerns the nature of the Church which is to perform this function. Is it enough that there should be vast numbers of Christian individuals gathering together in whatever way is proved by experience to be the most effective for edification, pursuing their profession as Christians, and so gradually leavening life? Or is there need for a quite definite society, with a coherent constitution and a known basis of membership? The former has much to recommend it; it avoids the deadening influence of a rigid machinery; it ensures freedom of spiritual and intellectual development; it may seem to correspond with that loosely constituted group of disciples, which was, as we have seen, the actual fruit of the earthly ministry of Christ. Yet it is condemned by all analogies, and is inadequate to the essential nature of religion.

All relevant analogy suggests that a spirit must take definite and concrete form before it can be effective in the world, even as God Himself must become incarnate in order to establish His Kingdom upon earth. No doubt the form has often fettered the spirit and sometimes even perverted it; the history of the Franciscan movement is an instance of this; but the influence of St. Francis would never have done for Europe what it actually accomplished if the Order had not been founded.

One of the clearest illustrations of the principle is before our eyes in our experience to-day. When the spirit of national patriotism makes its appeal, no one has to make any effort to understand its claim; our nation is a definite and concrete society in which we easily realise our membership to the full. We know that there is no escaping from it, and that, when it appeals for our service or our lives, we must either respond or refuse. But the Christian Church, as we know it, is powerless to bring home its appeal in the same way. Largely because of its divisions and endless controversy about the points, secondary though important, which separate the various sections, it has become curiously impotent in the face of any great occasion such as the present, and curiously unsuccessful in persuading either its own members or the world outside of the nature of its mission. We are not conscious, for example, that we are permanently either responding to, or else refusing, the appeal to "preach the Gospel to every creature." That appeal does not hit us personally as does the appeal, "every fit man wanted." Our membership in the Church does not in fact make us feel a personal obligation to assist the cause of the Church. We are content to "belong to it" without admitting that it has any power to dispose of its "belongings"; we think that we "support" it by "going to church" and contributing to "church expenses." But we feel no link with our fellow-Christians in Germany at all comparable to that which binds us to an agnostic but patriotic Englishman, or at all capable of bridging spontaneously the gulf fixed by national antagonism. By a deliberate effort we can realise that we and they are equally precious in the sight of God, and that they are our fellow-members in Christ. But there is no realised bond of corporate unity that binds us to each other, and we rely upon the very feeble resources of our personal good-will and personal faith for any sense of unity with them that we may attain. The Church is less powerful than the nation as an influence in our lives, partly at least because it is in fact less actual. The Church universal, whether as an organisation or as spirit of life, is an ideal, not a reality.

Such an argument, however, simply invites refutation. It is pointed out that when the whole of one section of Christendom was organised as a single religious community under the Pope, men did, as a mere matter of historical fact, fight and hate even more bitterly than now. A common membership in one Catholic Church did not prevent Edward III. and Henry V. from making war upon their neighbours across the English Channel. And at this moment Roman Catholic Frenchmen appear to be fighting against Roman Catholic Bavarians with no more signs of fellowship between the opponents than appear in other parts of the field of war. So far as the Church is organised as a unity, this does not, in fact, create unity of spirit in its members sufficient to mitigate national antagonisms.

And this, it will be urged, is only to be expected. "The wind bloweth where it listeth," and machinery cannot control the spirit. It is only a personal faith in Christ that will lift men above natural divisions so that they spontaneously recognise as brothers those who have similar faith. To build up again a great ecclesiastical organisation which shall include all Europe, or even all the world, will not of itself create friendship between the members who compose it if otherwise they are antagonistic. Individual conversion, not ecclesiastical statesmanship, is the one thing needful; nothing can take its place.

No; of course nothing can take its place. And of course an all-comprehensive lukewarm Church will share the fate of its smaller counterpart at Laodicea. When it is said that the Universal Church is not a reality, it is not only the absence of a world-wide organisation that is deplored; still worse is the total absence of any typical manner of life by which members of the Church may be known from others. Men die for Great Britain, not because Britain is a united kingdom, but because there is a definite British character which is ours and which we love. But there is no specifically Christian type of character actually distinguishing members of the Church from others which may make men ready to die for Christendom. Christians differ from others, as Spinoza bitterly remarked, not in faith or charity or any of the fruits of the Spirit, but only in opinion. Assuredly individual conversion is the primary requisite.

But half our troubles come from these absurd dilemmas. Do you believe in faith or in organisation? Well; do I believe in my eyes or my ears? Why not in both? Of course organisation cannot take the place of faith; of course faith without order is better than order without faith. But why cannot we have in the Church what we have got in the nation faith operative through order as loyalty is operative through the State and in service to it?

The earlier objection, however, is equally serious. Catholicism has failed in the past and is failing now. One main ground of its failure is to be found, I believe, in its inadequate recognition of nationality, which has avenged itself by almost ousting Catholicism, and with it Christianity itself, where national interests are concerned.[#]

[#] I am speaking throughout of the Western Church: the Eastern Church has perhaps been, if anything, too national.

This failure to give adequate recognition to nationality arises from too exclusive emphasis on the principle which is, quite rightly, the root idea of Catholicism—the idea of transcendence. Here in the last resort is the fundamental distinction between naturalism and religion; naturalism may take a form which stimulates the religious emotions and supports a high ethical ideal; but it confines itself to the limits of secular experience. For naturalism the history of man and of the universe is the starting-point and the goal; this as fact is the datum, this as understood is the solution. The Will of God, on this view, is to be discovered from the empirical course and tendency of history. But religion begins with God; it breaks in upon what we ordinarily call "experience" from outside; in its monotheistic form it regards the world as created by God for His own pleasure, and lasting only during that pleasure; in its pantheistic form it regards the world as a phase or a moment of His Being which is by no means limited to that phase or moment. Its philosophy does not elaborately conceive what God must be like in order to be the solution of our perplexities, but, starting with the assurance of His Being and Nature, shows how this is in fact the answer to all our needs.

It is one peculiarity and glory of Christianity that it unites both of those. Its faith is fixed upon One who "for us men and for our salvation came down from heaven," and who is yet the eternal Word through which all things were made, the indwelling principle of all existence. Transcendence and immanence are here perfectly combined. But because the former is the distinctively religious element, without which the latter would have been in danger of relapsing into naturalism, the deliberate emphasis was all laid on transcendence. We can see, as we look back, that when once the Incarnation has actually taken place upon the plane of history, it makes no jot of difference in logic, provided only that the Life of the Incarnate is taken as the starting-point and centre of thought, whether terms of transcendence or of immanence are used. The life of Christ is at once the irruption of the Divine into the world—(for the previous history of the world certainly does not explain it)—and is also the manifestation of the indwelling power which had all along sustained the world. In other words, the God who redeems is the same God who creates and sustains. But it is still true that the note of transcendence, of something given to man by God as distinct from something emerging out of man in his search of God, is the specifically religious note.

And the Church, as the divine creation and instrument, shares and must express this character. It must be so constituted as to keep alive this faith. That is the meaning of hierarchies and sacraments. Whether any given order is the most adequate that can be designed, is of course a perfectly legitimate question. But every order that aspires to be catholic aims, at least, at expressing the truth that religion is a gift of God, and not a discovery of man. And certainly it is only the gift of God that can be truly catholic or universal. Man's discoveries are indefinitely various; the European finds one thing, the Arab another, the Hindu yet another, and none finds satisfaction in the other's discovery, though in all of them God is operative. Only in His own gift of Himself is it reasonable to expect that all men will find what they need; only in a Church which is the vehicle of this gift, and is known to be this, and not a mutual benefit society organised by its own members for their several and collective advantage—only in a Church expressive of Divine transcendence can all nations find a home.

Yet just because of a too one-sided emphasis on this truth, the Catholic Church in the West has, as a rule, not tried to be a home for nations at all. "Christianity separated religion from patriotism for every nation which became, and which remained, Christian."[#] Patriotism is particular; religion ought to be universal. The nation is a natural growth; the Church is a divine creation. And so the primitive Church was organised in complete independence of national life, except in so far as its diocesan divisions followed national or provincial boundaries. No doubt the conditions of its existence made this almost necessary, for the organised secular life of the Roman Empire refused to tolerate it. But it was its own principle, true indeed but not the whole truth, which led to this line of development. The same principle is apparent in the Middle Ages, when there was no external pressure. The Church, as it was conceived in the sublime ideal of Hildebrand, was to belong to no nation, because supreme over them all, binding them together in the obedience and love of Christ, and imposing upon them His holy will.

[#] "War and Religion" in The Times Literary Supplement, Dec. 31, 1914.

The inevitable result of this was that the instinct of nationality was never christened at all. It remained a brute instinct, without either the sanction or the restraint of religion. But it could not be crushed, and so the Church let it alone; with the result that, though murder was regarded as a sin, a war of dynastic or national ambition was not by people generally considered sinful. No doubt theologians condemned such war in general terms; St. Thomas Aquinas, for instance, seems to regard as fully justified only such wars as are undertaken to protect others from oppression, and some of the greatest Popes made heroic efforts to govern national policy according to righteousness. But in the general judgment of the Church, international action was not subjected to Christian standards of judgment at all. This way of regarding the Church sometimes leads people to speak of "alternative" loyalties so that they ask, "Ought I to be loyal to my Church or to my nation?" And while faith and reason will combine to answer "To my Church," an imperious instinct will lead most men in actual fact to answer "To my nation." The attempt to exalt the Church to an unconditional supremacy has the actual result of making men ignore it when its guidance is most needed.

Whatever truth there may be in the statement that the Reformation was in part due to the growing sentiment of nationality, is evidence of the failure of the old Catholic Church in this matter. In England at any rate one main source of the popular Protestantism was the objection to anything like a foreign domination. No doubt the political ambitions of the Papacy were largely responsible for the feeling that the Catholic Church brought with it a foreign yoke. But the whole principle of the Church as non-national necessarily meant that the Church was regarded as "imposing" Christian standards rather than permeating national life with them. The Church tended to ignore the spiritual function of the State altogether, claiming all spiritual activity for itself alone; and thus it tended to make the State in actual fact unspiritual, and involved itself in the necessity of attempting what only the State can do. It thus not only tended to weaken the moral power of the State, but also forsook its own supernatural function to exercise those of the magistrate or judge, so that faith in the power of God was never put to a full test. The Reformation was not only a moral and spiritual reform of the Church, but the uprising of the nations, now growing fully conscious of their national life, against the cosmopolitan rule of Rome. But the Reformation did not fully realise its task. It expressed itself indeed in national Churches, but in actual doctrine tended to individualism; whereas Catholicism laid emphasis on religion as the gift of God, Protestantism, at least in its later development, laid stress on the individual's apprehension of the gift. But not only the individual—everything that is human, family, school, guild, trade union, nation, needs to apprehend and appropriate the gift of God. The nation, too, must be christened and submit to transforming grace.

The uprising of the national spirit has had the deplorable result of contributing to the break-up of Christendom, but it is not in itself deplorable at all. All civilisation has in fact progressed by the development of different nationalities, each with its own type. If we believe in a Divine Providence, if we believe that the life of Christ is not only the irruption of the Divine into human history but is also and therein the manifestation of the governing principle of all history, we shall confess that the nation as well as the Church is a divine Creation. The Church is here to witness to the ideal and to guide the world towards it, but the world is by divine appointment a world of nations, and it is such a world that is to become the Kingdom of God. Moreover, if it is by God's appointment that nations exist, their existence must itself be an instrument of that divine purpose which the Church also serves.

The whole course of Biblical revelation supports this view. It is quite true that if we were to read the New Testament for the first time, knowing nothing whatever about the Old, we should come to the conclusion that it almost entirely ignored nationality and everything which goes with it. But then the Church has always maintained that the New Testament grows by an organic life out of the Old, and presupposes it; and when we go back to that, there can be no doubt whatever about its view of nationality. The whole of the early books of the Old Testament are concerned with this, and almost nothing else. The task of Moses in the wilderness, of Joshua, of the Judges and the early Kings, is precisely to fashion Israel into a nation. So much is all attention concentrated upon this that we find a contentment with that contraction of the moral outlook which presents to many modern readers the chief stumbling block about the Old Testament. Almost everything that was serviceable to Israel is approved. Rahab is guilty of sheer treason to her own city of Jericho, but it is serviceable to Israel, and there is no word of condemnation. Jael is guilty of a very treacherous murder, but it was serviceable to Israel, so "Blessed shall she be above women in the tent."

Everything is concentrated upon this primary object of fashioning Israel into a nation and persuading individual Israelites to put the welfare of the whole before the interest and ambition of their own clique or faction; and when the time came for an advance to a wider view, it came precisely not by way of saying that national divisions do not matter and that national life itself is unimportant, but by insisting that nationality is equally precious in these other nations all around Israel as it is within Israel itself.

The turning point here as in so much else in the Old Testament is the Book of Amos, the first of the written prophecies. It is worth while to try to imagine the effect of those opening clauses. The prophet begins by securing a willing hearing from those to whom he writes: in other words he begins by abusing their neighbours.

And then, without a change of phrase, without even the compliment of a heightened denunciation—

[#] Amos i, 3-ii, 6.

It would be impossible more emphatically to insist that all nations, Israel and the rest, stand on an equal footing before the Judgment Seat of God, and are to be regarded as real entities, and real moral agents; but that is not enough for the prophet.

I have no more care for you than the Ethiopians—who then, as now, were black folk.

[#] Amos ix, 7.

It is the God who had guided the history of Israel who has equally guided the history of the despised Philistine and the hated Syrian. And this line of thought reaches its culmination where we should expect to find it, in the works of the statesman-prophet Isaiah. His little country of Judah was likely to be destroyed by the hostilities of Assyria and Egypt, and in the middle of that peril, when these nations were at each other's throats, he looks forward and says:—

There shall be free intercourse between them, and worship of the one God shall be the link between them.

[#] Isaiah xix, 23-25.

Just picture the pallid frenzy of the orthodox Jew at the words—"Egypt my people."

The teaching of the Bible is plain enough; and as we come to the New Testament, with all this in our minds, knowing the emphasis that has already been laid upon nationality, we find that there, too, is the note of patriotism.

No man has ever loved his nation more than the Lord loved Israel, and in the bitterness of disappointment in the lament over Jerusalem we have the measure of His patriotic love for the holy places of His people.

St. Paul, the author of those great ejaculations—"That there can be neither Jew nor Gentile, Greek nor Scythian, bond nor free, but one man in Christ Jesus"[#]—is also the author of the most ardent expression of patriotism in all literature.

[#] Gal. iii, 28; Col. iii, 11.

[#] Rom. ix, 1-5.

One can almost hear him panting as he dictates the words.

The Bible, then, strongly insists upon the nation as existing by divine appointment, and it looks forward, not to the abolition of national distinctions, but to the inclusion of all nations in the family of nations. So it was well that nationality should insist upon itself within the sphere of religion in the movement that we call the Reformation. But it left us with a broken Christendom, and with what are called national Churches. The old Church endeavoured to tyrannise over the State; under the influence of the Reformation the State tended to tyrannise over the Church. Then comes a movement towards a free Church in a free State; but we shall only find satisfaction when we have a free State in a free Church.

The nation is a natural growth with a spiritual significance. It emerges as a product of various elementary needs of man; but having emerged it is found to possess a value far beyond the satisfaction of these needs. The Church is a spiritual creation working through a natural medium. Its informing principle is the Holy Spirit of God in Christ, but its members are men and women who are partly animal in nature as well as children of God. The nation as organised for action is the State; and the State, being "natural," appeals to men on that side of their nature which is lower but is not in itself bad. Justice is its highest aim and force its typical instrument, though force is progressively less employed as the moral sense of the community develops: mercy can find an entrance only on strict conditions. The Church, on the other hand, is primarily spiritual; holiness is its primary quality; mercy will be the chief characteristic of its judgments, but it may fall back on justice and even, in the last resort, on force.[#] Both State and Church are instruments of God for establishing His Kingdom; both have the same goal; but they have different functions in relation to that goal.

[#] See .: On Moral Authority.

The State's action for the most part takes the form of restraint; the Church's mainly that of appeal. The State is concerned to maintain the highest standard of life that can be generally realised by its citizens; the Church is concerned with upholding an ideal to which not even the best will fully attain. When a man reaches a certain pitch of development, he scarcely realises the pressure of the State, though he is still unconsciously upheld by the moral judgment of society; but he can never outgrow the demand of the Church. On the other hand, if a man is below a certain standard, the appeal of the Church will not hold him and he needs the support of the State's coercion.

Neither State nor Church is itself the Kingdom of God, though the specific life of the Church is the very spirit and power of that Kingdom. Each plays its part in building the Kingdom, in which, when it comes, force will have disappeared, while justice and mercy will coalesce in the perfect love which will treat every individual according to his need.

The Church which, officially at least, ignored nationality has failed. The Church which allowed itself to become little more than the organ of national religion has failed. The hope of the future lies in a truly international Church, which shall fully respect the rights of nations and recognise the spiritual function of the State, thereby obtaining the right to direct the national States along the path which leads to the Kingdom of God. We are all clear by now that the Christian Church cannot be made the servant of one nation; we must become equally clear that it cannot be regarded as standing apart from them, so that in becoming a Churchman a man is withdrawn in some degree from national loyalty. We must get rid of the idea of "alternative" loyalties. The Church is indeed the herald and the earnest of that Kingdom of God which includes all mankind; but unless all history is a mere aberration, that Kingdom will have nations for its provinces, and nations like individuals will realise their destiny by becoming members of it.

We shall, then, conceive the relation of the nation to the Church on the analogy of that between the family and the nation. There is in principle no conflict of interest or loyalty here. The family is a part of the nation, owing allegiance to it; but the nation consists of families and can reach its welfare only through theirs. So the nation (in proportion as it is Christian) must learn to regard itself as a member of the family of nations in the Catholic Church. No doubt in this imperfect world there is often a conflict of supposed interests, and sometimes even of real interests. Moreover, there is often room for doubt as to where the true interest lies. But the family finds its own true welfare in the service of the nation, and the nation finds its own welfare in the service of the Kingdom of God.

The Catholic Church, which is itself not yet a society of just men made perfect, while upholding the ideal of brotherhood and the love which kills hate by suffering at its hands, and while calling both men and nations to penitence and renewed aspiration in so far as they fail to reach that ideal, will none the less recognise the divinity of the nation in spite of all its failures. It will not call upon men to come out from their nation or separate themselves from its action, unless it believes that then and there the nation itself is capable of something better, or unless the nation requires of them a repudiation of the very spirit of Christ, or an action intrinsically immoral. If it is doing the best that at the moment it is capable of doing, the Church will bid its citizens support it in that act, lest the nation be weakened in its defence of the right or its control handed over to those who have no care for the right.

The Church then must recognise the nation having a certain function in the divine providence with reference to man's spiritual life. It must not try to usurp the State's functions, for if it does it will perform them badly, and it will also—which is far more serious—be deserting the work for which it alone is competent; and the State must, in its turn, recognise the Church as the Society of Nations, of which it with all others is a member.

Nothing but such a spiritual society can secure fellowship among nations. Schemes of arbitration, conciliation, international police and the like, presuppose, if they are to be effective, an admitted community of interest between the nations. But this must be not only admitted but believed in sufficiently to prompt a nation which has no interest in a particular dispute to make sacrifices for the general good, by spending blood and treasure in upholding the authority of the international court or council. What will secure this, except the realisation of common membership in the Kingdom of God, and in the Christian Church, its herald and earnest?

And yet the Church we know is not only divided but at war within itself. This, the Creation of God in Christ, is not more free from strife and faction than the nations, which are natural growths. If grace fails, how can nature succeed? Why should we expect the nations of the world to be at peace, when the sections of the Church are at war?

Because the Church is so far from what we hope it may become, we can only sketch that future Church in outline. Its building will be the work of years, perhaps of centuries. And probably enough our attempt will fail as Hildebrand's failed; probably enough there will be scores of failures; but each time we must begin again in order that for Christ and His Spirit a Body may be prepared, through which His purpose may in the end of the ages find its accomplishment, and the nations of the earth bring their glory—each its own—into His Holy City.

There is the goal; dimly enough seen; but the method is perfectly plain. "Thomas saith unto Him, Lord, we know not whither Thou goest; how know we the way? Jesus saith unto him, I am the way." And when that way led to the Cross, beside the innocent Sufferer there were two others. One cried to Him, "Save Thyself and us"; the other recognised His royalty in that utmost humiliation and prayed, "Jesus, remember me when Thou comest in Thy Kingdom." He, and he alone in the four Gospels, is recorded to have addressed the Lord by His personal name. Penitence creates intimacy, whether it be offered to God or to man.

We have been made very conscious of the burden of the world's pain and sin, though perhaps that burden, as God bears it, is no heavier now than in our selfish and worldly peace. Will the Church pray to Him, "Save Thyself and us"? or will it willingly suffer with Him, united with Him in the intimacy of penitence, seeing His royalty in His crown of thorns? Will it, while bidding men bravely do their duty as they see it, still say that the real treasures are not of this world though they may in part be possessed here, suffering whatever may be the penalty for this unpopular testimony? For the kingdoms of this world will become the Kingdom of our God and of His Christ only when the citizens of those kingdoms lay up their treasure in heaven and not upon the earth, only when, being risen with Christ, they set their affection on things above— love, joy, peace, loyalty, beauty, knowledge—only when they realise their fellowship in His Body so that their fellowship also in His Holy Spirit may purge their selfishness away.

Here is field enough for heroism and the moral equivalent of war. The Church is to be transformed and become a band of people united in their indifference to personal success or national expansion, and caring only that the individual is pure in heart and the nation honourable. In her zeal for that purity and honour, and in her contempt for all else, she may have to suffer crucifixion. It is a big risk that the Church must run; for if she does not save the world she will have ruined it, besides sacrificing herself. If there is no God nor Holy City of God, the Church will have just spoilt life for all her faithful members, and in some degree for every one else as well. But if her vision is true, then everything is worth while—rather the greatness of the sacrifice is an addition to the joy when the prize is so unimaginably great. Can we bring this spirit into the Church? On our answer depends the course of history in the next century, and a new stage in the Coming of the Lord.

LECTURE III

JUSTICE AND LIBERTY IN THE STATE

"Think not that I came to destroy the law or the prophets: I came not to destroy but to fulfil."—S. Matthew v., 17.

I.—In the last lecture I said that justice would seem to be the typical virtue of the State, as holiness of the Church. Let us, then, first consider this virtue of justice in the light of our Lord's teaching concerning one of the most familiar aspects of justice—its penal aspect.

Those sayings that have of late given rise to so many searchings of heart among Christians—the sayings about turning the other cheek and the rest—are given by our Lord as explanations of the saying that He came "not to destroy the law but to fulfil it." The words "to fulfil" of course mean not only to obey and carry out, but to complete.

In what sense is this teaching of our Lord the completion of the law? For the law of Moses, like every other law, was concerned with regulating the relations of men to one another, as well as their duties towards God; and it enforced what it enjoined by penalties.

At first sight no doubt it looks as if He were directly contradicting what had been said to them of old time—

How is this the fulfilment or completion of the Mosaic or any other law? At this distance of time, it is hard to remember what was the original significance of the law of retaliation. We are inclined to think that the words "an eye for an eye and a tooth for a tooth" are intended to give a licence to that degree of vindictiveness; but on the contrary, in the primitive stage in which that enactment was given, it was not a licence given to man's instinct for vengeance, but a limitation set upon that primitive and animal instinct, whose natural tendency, if unchecked, is to take two eyes for an eye and a set of teeth for a tooth. The lex talionis said—Only an eye for an eye, and only a tooth for a tooth.

Our Lord carries the same principle further; not even that degree of vindictiveness is allowed. The first necessity was to put bounds upon man's natural and almost insatiable lust for vengeance. The next was to tell him that the whole method of vengeance could never succeed in what is its only really justifiable aim. For what is the true function of the law, whether that of Moses or any other? It is always two-fold; it must always aim not merely at checking the evil act, but at converting, if possible, the evil will.

There has never, I suppose, been any legal system which was not justified by its upholders on this ground. No one is really content, to think that the punishment which he inflicts, or may imagine himself as inflicting through the agency of the State, or in any other way, is purely deterrent; he always thinks it will also be reformative. But, how are you as a matter of fact to attack the evil will? The mere infliction of penalty will not of any necessity achieve this goal at all. We know that it is very seriously debated whether our whole system of punishment in the civilised States of to-day has any really moral effect, at least upon those who fall under its most severe penalties. Probably most convicts leave prison worse men than when they entered. For if a man is below a certain level in moral attainment, pain, far from purifying, only brutalises and coarsens. It is only those who are already far in the path of spiritual growth who are purified by suffering, even as the Captain of our Salvation was thus made perfect. But it is still true that the aim of all penal law is twofold; to check the evil act and, if possible, to convert the evil will.

Now, as I suggested previously, mere restraint may have indirectly a positive moral value; as for example in the case of a child, who is potentially of very diverse characters. He has the capacity to grow in many different directions, and it will depend very much upon his surroundings, and the influences which play upon his character, whether this set of instincts or that receives development; and here merely to keep forcibly within bounds the development of certain impulses, which tend to grow out of proportion to the proper harmony and economy of nature, may indirectly have the effect of preserving that harmony and thus develop genuine virtue in the soul. And again, with those whose characters are relatively formed, the direct restraint, for example, of State action may have positive moral value, inasmuch as it is the expression of the moral judgment of Society. What most of us would shrink from, if we were in danger of imprisonment, would not be the physical inconvenience, which is not very great, but the fact that we should have brought ourselves under the censure of Society, and acted in such a way as to put ourselves below the level which Society generally considers itself justified in enforcing. And so the purely restraining influence of the State, even operating through force, may have a positive moral value, because it represents, and is the only way at present devised of representing, the judgment of Society, and to shrink from the judgment of Society is, so far as it goes, a really moral fear. It is not indeed the highest ground for the avoidance of evil, but it is a moral ground, for it arises from our recognition of our fellow-membership in Society with those whose censure we fear.

But the State in all its actions is of necessity mechanical, and cannot take account of the individual, and all that makes him what he is. The State officer cannot know the prisoner in such a way as really to determine the treatment allotted to him in the light of what is best for his spiritual welfare; and therefore he has to fall back upon rough and ready rules which will never be perhaps very far from the right treatment, though they may fail to allot the ideal treatment in any single case. And here, in parenthesis, let me just mention that this is the chief reason why metaphors and comparisons drawn from the law-courts are so sadly misleading when used to illustrate the relation between the human soul and God; our only fear of the judge is concerned with what he will do to us; but what we fear with our father, on earth or in Heaven, is not so much what he will do to us, as the pain we have caused—"There is mercy with Thee; therefore shalt Thou be feared."

Our Lord's method is the only one that aims straight at the evil will; it is the only method which has in it any real hope of converting the individual. It may fail time and again; but it is the only one that has a chance of real and absolute success.

Let us look for a moment at the instances which He chooses to illustrate the principle, and we shall see at once that they are carefully chosen. All the acts chosen are such as are particularly vexatious to the ordinary natural and selfish man—being struck in the face; having a vexatious suit brought against one; being pestered by a beggar; being compelled to do something for the public service when we are busy. Those are just the things which the natural man resents and which the real Christian will not mind at all. For, after all, there is no real injury in being struck in the face, or having one's coat taken away. What one minds is the insult to one's precious dignity; and the Christian who, by definition, has forgotten all about himself will not mind such injuries at all. Therefore if the acts commanded are spontaneously done and not done with a laborious conscientiousness—that is to say if they are done in the spirit of Christianity, and not in the spirit of Pharisaism—they will express a complete conversion in the will of him who does them; they will express absolute conquest of self, and a concern solely for the welfare of him with whom we are dealing; and there is no heart yet made that can resist the appeal of love which is constant in spite of every betrayal, the appeal of trust which is renewed in spite of endless disappointments.

"He that loveth his brother"—says St. John—"walketh in the light." He is the man who knows where he is going, because he is the man who understands people and sees into their hearts. They will reveal to him secrets of their nature, which they will hide from the contemptuous and indifferent; and even if at first he is from time to time disappointed and betrayed, in the end his method will succeed, because love and trust create what they believe in.

The justice then, which we find at work in the State, is always a provisional thing pointing us to something more, something which the State itself by its very constitution is unable to provide, but which God provides in Christ, and will enable us in our measure to provide, if we are faithful, at least in the circle of our immediate activities, so far, that is, as the range of our sympathy will carry us.

II.—The value of the justice which the State is able to secure actually resides for the most part in the liberty which it makes possible. Justice, as the State interprets it, is of itself, as far as I can see, almost totally valueless. I can see no kind of advantage in merely allotting so much pain to so much evil. There is moral evil in a man and you put physical evil into him as well. I do not see how you have made him or anyone else the better. Only in so far as the punishment is either deterrent or reformative, has it any moral value at all; and only in the latter case, where it reforms the character, can the value be called in the strict sense moral. So far as it only deters men from evil acts which they would desire to commit, it may add to the convenience of the other members of Society, but it is not doing any direct moral good.

Indirectly, however, it has moral results; for when we enquire in what sense we can say that such justice as the State secures produces liberty, the first answer is to be found in the obvious and elementary fact that the liberty of every one of us depends upon our knowledge that certain impulses and instincts in other people, should they arise, will be checked and not allowed to receive full expression. Our liberty is increased by that check put upon predatory or homicidal impulses in other people, and their liberty depends upon the suppression of such impulses in us.

So far it would seem that there must be in the most obvious sense of the words a certain curtailment of everybody's liberty in order that anybody may have liberty at all. If we are all to be free to indulge our passions of anger and hatred, should such arise within us, then it is quite clear that there will be very little freedom of action in the Society which rests on that principle. Everyone will go about in fear of everyone else.

But that is a very small part of the business. The chief contribution of such justice to human liberty is that it supplies the necessary conditions of discipline without which there can be no liberty. We think of liberty as meaning freedom from external constraint. We think that an act of ours is free when we can say, "I did it, and no one made me do it"; but very little reflection is sufficient to convince us that a man whose life is actually governed by one or several over-developed passions which he will, as a matter of fact, always gratify when opportunity offers, in spite of the damage that is done to his whole life and to his permanent and deliberate purpose, is not really a free man. To be tied and bound with the chain of our sins is just as much slavery as to be in the ownership of another man; and we can acquire the real liberty which is worth having, the liberty, that is, to shape our lives, to live according to our own purpose, following out our own ideal, only in so far as our natures have been welded by discipline into unity, so that we are no longer a chaos of impulses and instincts, any of which may be set in motion by the appropriate environment, but are self-governing persons controlling our own lives.

Liberty, in so far as it is of any value, always means self-control in both the senses of that term: in the sense that we are only controlled by ourselves, and also in the sense that by ourselves we are controlled, and that every part of our nature is subservient to the purpose to which our whole nature is given. Legislation is really an instrument of self-discipline. The people who write books about political philosophy are mainly members of the respectable classes. They naturally find it rather difficult to envisage themselves as liable to commit murder and the like; and they are therefore very liable to represent the criminal law of the State as being enacted against a few undisciplined or recalcitrant members. But when we look at the thing more closely, we see that what a community does, especially a democratic community, when it passes a law, is to invoke, every member upon his own head, the penalties enacted by that law, if he should do the act which the law forbids.

Let us consider, for example, an international convention. What is the use of nations agreeing with one another not to do something, for instance not to poison wells, unless there is some chance that in a moment of strong temptation they may desire to do it? They therefore strengthen their deliberate purpose to avoid such acts by entering into an agreement with one another always to avoid them. There would be no object in doing this unless they needed help, or thought that they might at some time need help, in living up to their own purposes.

And we have to remember that in this way the law of the State is, as a matter of fact, perpetually operating upon every one of us. We are often liable to suppose that it is only active in relation to those people against whom it is definitely set in motion; but it does operate in the life of every one of the citizens of a community; because the fact that certain actions would involve us in State-penalty most undoubtedly does keep all of us from indulging in those actions at certain times, even though at calm moments we recognise that it would be wrong to do so. Trivial instances are nearly always the clearest. Most of us, I suppose, are sufficiently honest to desire in general terms to pay for what we buy; and we should perhaps usually pay for our places in the train, even if there were no ticket-inspector; still, the existence of the inspector just clinches the matter.[#] The possibility of the penalty as a matter of fact helps to maintain our general, permanent, and deliberate purpose of honesty against a momentary temptation to be dishonest; and so far it is helping us to live up to our purpose, or, in other words, is increasing our real freedom. In fact, one main test of good legislation is precisely whether it does or does not in this way develop real freedom by increasing people's power to live by their own deliberate purpose.

[#] I owe the illustration to Mr. A. L. Smith, of Balliol.

Now so far we have been considering Society as consisting of relatively free persons (though the freedom exists in varying degrees, both as regards the external constraint and capacity for self-control), these persons having various claims which have to be regulated by the justice which the State upholds; in other words, in this stage, we are regarding justice in the way in which I suppose it is most usually regarded, namely, as rendering to a man what is due to him. That is the definition with which Plato in The Republic starts his enquiry, and he naturally found very soon that it would not work.[#] It will not work because the moral values of people are not determinable. You cannot, as a matter of fact, ever say what is the relative weight of the various claims that may be made on behalf of this or that man. Most particularly there is the perpetual conflict between the actual and the potential worth of any men.

[#] He appropriately puts it in the mouth of Polemarchus, the well-brought up, but wholly inexperienced, young man.

Suppose that we decide that we will give to all men in Society that which is their due. How are we going to determine what is due? Is it to be determined by their economic value, for example by the amount they are contributing to the economic or general welfare of Society? Well then, there are a large number of people at both ends of what we call the social scale who ought to receive nothing at all, because they are contributing nothing economically, or, indeed, in any other way, to the public welfare. And yet that is not their fault; they have been brought up, it may be in squalor, it may be in luxury, but in either case in circumstances which have made them almost incapable of anything like good citizenship. Are we to kill such persons, or leave them to starve, in the interest of the public welfare? All human instincts will protest that this is unjust, and that they can claim more than they can possibly be represented as contributing, simply because they have had, as we say, bad luck, and it is not their fault.[#]

[#] See , On Justice and Education.

Let us try what happens if after Plato's example we turn the matter upside down, and instead of saying that justice will be found when there is rendered to each man what is due to him, we say that justice is found when each man contributes what is due from him.

Now logically, of course, these two are the same, because duties and rights are absolutely correlative. My rights constitute other people's duties towards me, and their rights constitute my duties towards them. The only difference is that it is far more easy in any given case to determine what is due from somebody—what can be claimed from him—than to determine what is due to him.

In this imperfect stage of the world, where we are passing through the transition from something like barbarism to Christian civilisation, as we hope, it is possible that of two correlative processes, one will actually carry us further than the other even though it is logically inseparable from it. And in fact we find at once, that if we put it this way, and say that the principle of justice is not that each man should obtain what is due to him, but that each should contribute what is due from him, we are coming to the central principle of God's administration of His world, which is that we should render to every man not according to his desert, but according to his need. Indeed for practical purposes, if we are wishing to bring justice into our own dealings, and into the dealings of any public body with which we may have influence, this principle will carry us further than any other—"Render to every man according to his need."

Let us suppose that we meet on one day with two beggars. One of them is a man who has borne a good character throughout his life, and has lost his work through no fault of his own; the works on which he was employed were closed, and he is now tramping in search of more work. All of us of course will say—"He deserves help and we will help him." Yes; and it is quite easy to help him. We have only to set him up again, and all will be well. It is not his own fault and we can rely upon him to make use of another opportunity. The other beggar is a man who has lost this place, as he has lost many before, through indulgence in some vice, such as drink. There are very many people who will say, "Well, it is his own fault, and now he must suffer for it." If God had taken that line with us, where would our redemption be?—"It is his own fault, now he must suffer for it." To say that is to repudiate the Gospel in its entirety. It is to call the Cross absurd and scandalous. "God commendeth His love toward us in that while we were yet sinners Christ died."

No; the Christian will say, "This man needs help more than the other." It will not be the same kind of help. It is no use merely to give him money. That may merely help him to go wrong quicker than he would otherwise. He needs something that will cost us, probably, more than money; he needs our time—time to make friends; time to remove his suspicions; time to enter into real sympathy with him, and to detect what elements of strength there are in his character, that we may build them up again. But he needs help more than the other, and the Christian will be bound to give it, and he will say—"It was his own fault; he cannot help himself; it depends entirely on us; we will render to him according to his need."

And all of this would lead to another formula for describing the justice which we shall desire to practise in the State, and in all our secular life of which the State is the highest organisation— The recognition of personality.

I do not know at all what forms your labour unrest in takes in this continent, but I claim to have considerable opportunities of knowing what is the root of that unrest in England, at least among the better type of working people; for I am concerned with an organisation which is at work among working folk all over England, having an enormous membership, and which aims at claiming for them, and supplying them with, further facilities for education. Those with whom I thus come in contact are picked men, no doubt, because those who join an educational association are thereby marked off at once as intellectually at least more alert than those who do not join; but as I go about them, I find no room whatever for doubting that the root of the labour unrest in England is a sense that the whole organisation of our life constitutes a standing insult to the personality of the poor man. Why, for example, he feels, should it be possible for a well-to-do man to secure for himself, or for his wife, or for his child, the medical attendance that may be needed, while he in very many parts of our country depends upon institutions maintained by voluntary contributions? It is quite compatible with gratitude to those whose generosity maintains these institutions to feel that for such service he should not be dependent upon anybody's charity at all—whether the solution is to be that the State maintain such institutions or that every man who is doing his fair share of the country's work receive for himself the wage that will enable him to deal with such emergencies as they arise.

Above all, men feel the denial of their personality in the organisation of industry itself. Men have fought and died for political liberty, which means the right to have a voice in making the laws by which you are to be governed. But the laws of the State do not for the most part invade a man's home, whereas the regulations of an industrial firm do. They determine when he shall get up in the morning and when he shall go to bed; they determine whether he shall have any leisure for the pursuit of any interest of his own. In the making of those regulations he has, as a rule, no voice whatever, and no opportunity of making his views understood except by threat, the threat of a strike. The men feel that they are what they are sometimes called, "hands" not persons. They are the tools of other men. You must apply all this to your own country, if and so far as it does apply. But one might easily imagine a village in Lancashire, or any other industrial district where all the inhabitants are dependent upon one industry; there are many such; and the control of that industry may be in the hands of a Board of Directors, settled perhaps in London; it may only meet a few times a year for the transaction of business, and otherwise not exist at all. They never see the people whose lives and destinies they thus control. The shareholders who want their dividends make no enquiries as a rule about the conditions in which the work is done. If that Board of Directors mismanages its business the village in Lancashire goes hungry. If that Board of Directors, when they have already got a full supply of work, takes on another large contract, that village in Lancashire works overtime; and the people have no say in the matter. Whatever else that is, it is not liberty, and in the judgment of the people themselves it is not justice. And indeed it is not either justice or liberty as we have learned in other spheres to understand those terms. The economic organisation of life comes far closer to the individual citizen than the political organisation, and the development of justice remains incomplete until it has secured liberty of an economic as well as a political kind.

If it is true that the method of Christ is to appeal to the free personality of the man, so that he obeys out of love and devotion and not from fear of penalty nor hope of reward, other than the reward of realising the love of the Master, then surely it is in the true line of development towards the perfected Christian civilisation if we demand that these opportunities for the development of free personality shall be afforded. No doubt it must be done with wisdom. Rough and ready methods, however well-meant, might do far more harm than good, and leave us in a situation even worse than that which we know. But the Church has paid scarcely any attention to those things in England. It is very difficult to persuade Church-people that, because they are followers of Christ, and therefore might be assumed to recognise that they are "members one of another" with all these others, they are therefore bound (for example) in investing their money to find out the conditions under which their dividends are going to be earned. In almost every department of life we have left such things alone. Under the stress of war, we have suddenly become acutely conscious of the drink evil. It was there before; and we have been content that the great majority of our fellow citizens should have no opportunity for gratifying those instincts of social life and merriment, which are the birthright of all God's children, except in places where the influence of alcohol was supreme. We have been content with that. We have not thought it was our duty to find a means of supplying them with other places of recreation and amusement; we have saved our money. And then we have the impertinent audacity to claim our own redemption by the blood of Christ.

One can go on with one evil after another in the same way. This is what makes the Church weak. It is no sort of use for us to say that Christ is the Redeemer of the world, and the Revealer of the way of life, if with regard to just those evils which press most heavily on men we have to say that for them He has unfortunately not supplied a remedy.

No doubt if these evils are to be dealt with on a large scale, the work must be done by the State, for nothing else is adequate; and the Church here has two main tasks. It is no part of the Church's task to advocate general principles or particular maxims of economic science, though its members, in their capacity of citizenship ought to be active in these ways. The first task of the Church is to inspire the State, which after all very largely consists of the same persons as itself, with the desire to combat the evil; and the second is to counteract the one great difficulty which the State experiences. When the State takes up such work as this, there is one thing which we all fear: "Officialism." What is "Officialism"? Simply lack of love; nothing else in the world. It consists in treating people as "cases," according to rules and red tape, instead of treating them as individuals; and the Church which must inspire the State to want to deal with these things, must then supply the agents through whom it may deal with them effectively, inspiring them with the love of men which is the fruit and test of a true love of God.

But beyond all this, the Church must be making demands far greater than it has ever made upon man's spiritual nature and spiritual capacity, and must then point to the organisation of our social life and say—"That organisation, because and in so far as it deprives men of the full growth of their spiritual nature, because and in so far as it prevents them from taking the share which belongs to God's children in His worship and the enjoyment of his gifts of nature and Grace, is proved to be of the devil."

In our worship we find for the most part what we expect to find. There may be gifts offered us, gifts from God, that we never receive because we have not looked for them. It is in our intercourse with Christ that we shall find the means of solving the horror of our social problem, if we are expecting to find it; but we have not expected it. We have not really believed that He is the Redeemer of the World; we have not looked to Him for the redemption of Society. The State by itself, until the Church comes to its help, can do something indeed, but something which by itself is almost worthless.[#] It supplies the indispensable foundation without which a spiritual structure cannot be built up; but, if that building never comes, the foundation by itself is little more than useless. To those whom the social order favours it offers real liberty and life, but no inspiration; a perfect social order would offer liberty to all, but still no inspiration. The State alone can never be the house of many mansions wherein every soul is truly at home.

[#] It is to be observed that the State is by its very nature largely limited to the regulation of those human relationships where men oppose each other with rival claims; as soon as men rise to the reciprocity of friendship the method of the State is inappropriate. People do not go to law to determine whether either loves the other adequately.

LECTURE IV

HOLINESS AND CATHOLICITY IN THE CHURCH

"This is the law of the house: upon the top of the mountain the whole limit thereof round about shall be most holy. Behold, this is the law of the house."—Ezekiel xliii, 12.

"And I saw no temple therein: for the Lord God Almighty, and the Lamb, are the temple thereof."—Revelation xxi, 22.

The Bible gives us two elaborately conceived pictures of the perfected life of man. The first is that which occupies the closing chapters of Ezekiel's prophecy; its leading feature is the immense separation which is insisted upon between the Temple and the secular City. The Hill of Zion has become a very high mountain; upon the top of it the Temple is set, and there is a wide space, at least two miles, between it and the City of Jerusalem, which has been moved away by that distance to the south.

Indeed, if we take the description as intended to be complete, the City seems to exist chiefly to provide a congregation for the Temple's services, and the Prince only to offer representative worship on behalf of His people. All attention is concentrated upon the place of the worship of God, and the holiness which is to be characteristic of that place. By thus keeping the Temple holy, through separating it from the body of the City and its secular life, the Prophet attains no doubt the end he has in view, but he also, of necessity, though probably unintentionally, leaves the suggestion that the secular life itself cannot be wholly consecrated.

In sharp contrast with this is St. John's picture in the Book of Revelation; here there is no specific place of worship at all, for the whole City is the Temple of God; more than that, the whole City is the very Holy of Holies, for it is described as being a perfect cube, and the Holy of Holies in Solomon's Temple was a perfect cube.

[#] Rev. xxi, 16, 17.

The City thus corresponds in symbolic form with the Holy of Holies. It is become the dwelling place of God. No special shrine is needed, no place to which men draw apart, because their whole life is an act of worship, and God dwells among them in their daily activities.

There is one feature about this Heavenly City, which is obscured through the use of the old terms of measurement, for this cube is described as being 1,500 miles high, 1,500 miles broad, and 1,500 miles long; but the wall which stands for defence against foes without and for the containment and order of the life within, and indeed represents in general the principle of organisation—the wall is only 216 feet high; so small a thing is order in comparison with the life which it safeguards.

It is between those two poles, which are set for us as the extreme terms in a process, that the Church must live its life. There is truth in both of them.

We were considering in the last lecture justice and liberty, which are the supreme achievements of the National State. Let us to-day consider the Holiness and Catholicity, which are the supreme treasures of the Church.

Holiness must come first, Holiness which means absolute conformity to the will of God. Whatever obstacles there may be to overcome, whatever seductions to avoid, the Church is to remain absolutely devoted to the Divine Will. Only so can it be catholic or universal. It might for a moment achieve an all-embracing unity by giving up everything that is offensive to men, and gathering all within it under the glow of a comfortable sentiment; but then its life would be gone, and after a little while the men who had all become members of it would be just as though they had not. Only a Church which is perfectly loyal to the Will of God, can possibly be the home for all mankind.

But Holiness has always had two meanings—an outward and an inward, a ceremonial and a moral. We shall agree, I suppose, in saying that the outward and ceremonial is in itself of no consequence, and exists only in order to preserve and make possible the inward and spiritual conformity to God's Will; but for that purpose, as all human experience has always shown, it is quite indispensable. We are made of bodies as well as souls, and if our whole being is to be permeated, there must be bodily expression of that which our souls enjoy or need. We must worship with our bodies as well as with our souls. So St. Paul, after all his emphasis upon the spirit as against dead works, begins his practical exhortation with the words, "I beseech you, therefore, brethren, by the mercies of God to present your bodies a living sacrifice."[#] The physical and bodily expression is always necessary, in this human life of ours, to the full efficacy and to the survival through the ages of the spiritual, though this no doubt is alone of ultimate consequence.

[#] Rom. xii, 1.

If the Church is to maintain its Holiness, it must of necessity be to some extent separated from the world; it cannot mix as a Church in all worldly activities. It cannot simply set itself out to permeate the general life of men, maintaining nothing that is separate and apart for itself. If it does that, it will simply be lost in the general life of the world.

In the last resort our characters depend almost entirely upon the influences that play upon them in our environment; the one place where we have effective choice is in determining the influences to which we will submit ourselves. If there is no place in our society, or in the world, where men may count upon finding the power of God in purity, then men will inevitably fail to rise above that sort of character, which their worldly environment happens to be forming in them.

The Church then, precisely in order to do this work in the world, must keep itself in some sense separate from the world; but the vast majority of its members are people in the daily life of the world, pursuing their avocations there; and it would plainly be wholly disastrous to require that all Christian people, in virtue of their Christianity, should withdraw themselves from the ordinary concerns of men.

There is, therefore, no means by which this separateness of the Church can be achieved unless there are certain persons set apart to be representatives of the Church, and of the Church only; and who, because they are official representatives of the Church are thereby deprived of the right to take part in many worldly activities, though these in themselves are right enough.

It is not because they are more truly members of the Church than others, nor because there is a different moral standard for clergy and laity, but because in the whole life of the Church there are certain functions which are incompatible with others, just as in the State a man cannot be at the same time an advocate and a judge, or commander-in-chief and ambassador.

Thus, for example, as it seems to me, one who is called to be a priest of the Church, inevitably forfeits the right to take part in the hurly-burly of party politics; partly because, in a world which consists of many parties, he is responsible for bringing before men the claim of God to which all the parties ought to bow; partly also because a man's activities inevitably affect the quality of his own mind, and if we are to be as it were repositories of the Eternal truths, if we are to have ready for dispensation all the treasures which God commits to His Church, we need a type of mind which cannot, at least by most men, be maintained, if we are engaged in heated controversy and frequent debate.

Another example may be found in the question whether a priest should serve as a combatant in his country's army. He is called to represent the Church; and the Church is essentially, not accidentally, international; it is not international merely as a scientific society may be, in that it is not concerned with political frontiers and men of all nations are welcome within it; but it is international in the sense that it exists to bind the nations of the earth in one. The officer of such a society may be as patriotic in his feeling as anyone else, but, just because he is an official, for him to take positive action on one side of the other weakens the Church's international position, and is, therefore, a more serious act than it is in the case of the layman. Here again there are not two standards, but there are diverse circumstances. If the Church called on all its members to refuse to serve, the result would be to interfere with the freedom of the State to act in its own sphere; if it allows everyone to serve, it is deprived of its Catholic witness just when that is most vitally needed. The only way of doing justice to the legitimate claims of both nationalism and Catholicity, is to differentiate between persons; and there is no practicable or even sensible way of doing this except to make the Church's officers responsible for the Catholic witness and its lay, or unofficial, members for the national.

But does this not involve the danger of a priestly caste? Yes, no doubt it does; but there are two ways in which we may avoid falling into that danger. The first is perpetually to remember that men are called by God to the different kinds of work which He has for them to do; and we shall avoid unctuousness, which is no doubt what men most dread about a priestly caste, if we keep it perpetually in our mind that we are not personally holy because our calling is. We are entrusted with this great charge. We have to fulfil it. It is our work for Him. But there are those whom He calls to serve Him as politicians and as soldiers; if they do their work as in His sight, and to His glory, they are serving Him every bit as much as we are. All the work of all the kinds of men is needed in the world, and it is only if we suppose that we are made more holy because our calling is concerned with the specifically holy things that we shall fall before that danger.

And the other safeguard, paradoxical as it may sound, is a very complete specialised training. One of the reasons, I am quite sure, why lay people often find us rather stilted and uncongenial is because we have not secured a sufficient grasp upon what is our own special subject to feel full liberty in conversation and to speak naturally. We are perpetually wondering at what point we shall be suddenly compromising that for which we are responsible. We tend to utter (and even to hold) merely conventional opinions and to express ourselves only in the stereotyped phrases, because we have not sufficient grasp of spiritual and moral truth to trust ourselves in forming individual opinions, or in finding our own language for expressing the opinions which we form. Precisely in the degree in which we know our own work and have full possession of what is entrusted to us, shall we obtain liberty and ease of manner, and be in general behaviour just like other people, which is what we ought most to desire.

Still it is in the person of its priests that the Church must maintain that outward holiness, that separation from the world, which alone makes possible a concentration upon things divine; and without this concentration it can never become a catholic or universal body. "Universal," here does not, of course, mean all-inclusive. There are those who definitely and deliberately reject the claim of Christ, and those have never been submitted in any way to His influence. The unbaptized heathen are not members of the Catholic Church; and if they refuse the Gospel when it comes, they remain outside. Moreover, as we have seen, there is possible a vicious as well as a holy catholicity. There is nothing so seductive as the temptation to suppose that doctrine which evokes a response is on that account true, or particularly to be emphasised. Sometimes people dislike the truth. There are people who are alienated by it; and the attractiveness of our gospel to people, irrespective of their frame of mind, is no evidence of its divinity. There is a picture in the Old Testament where Moses the Prophet is apart upon the mountain top, communing with God, while at the foot of the mountain, Aaron, the official priest, is ministering to the people the kind of religion they like. He was encouraging them, as the Psalmist satirically says, to worship: "the similitude of the calf that eateth hay." There was nothing very dignified about it. But it was what the people liked; and the response to his ministrations was immediate and immense. Our task is to lay hold, so far as we may in our infinite feebleness, of the truth that was given to the world in Christ in all its sternness as well as its love—or rather in that sternness which is an essential part of its love; and this is what we must present to men.

Again, it is not in proportion to their virtue in the ordinary moral sense that men are drawn to the Church; it is in proportion to their conscious need of God. It is perhaps worth while just now especially to emphasise the peril of a faithless virtue, and the depth of error involved in any attempt to take for the basis of a Church "the religion of all good men." What will happen to a man who sets his effort upon the building up of his whole character according to an ethical ideal? One of two things. Either he may in part succeed, perhaps as much as he himself desires to succeed, and then he may become self-satisfied and a Pharisee; or else he will find himself either failing altogether, or, having succeeded in part, incapable of carrying the success to its full completion, and not knowing where to find the power that will take him further; and so he ends in despair.

No, the appeal of the Church, as universal, is simply that it has within it that which answers the real and deepest need of every human being. There everyone will find his home, when once he has found his need of God, if indeed the Church is holy.

And this is also its distinction from the sects; for it endeavours to uphold the entire body of the truth, every particle of it that may be of service to anyone. I suppose there are very few of us to whom the whole of the Creed is a living reality. We may believe it all, but what we live by is usually a small part of it, and it is a different part with different persons. The essence of sectarianism, as I understand it, is the gathering together of those people who live by the same part of the Creed, in order that, like mingling with like, they may develop a great intensity and fervour of devotion. For a moment, indeed, they may be far more effective than the great body of the Church, and yet they cannot become universal. There is something lacking from what they uphold, which someone needs.[#] The aim of the Church is to be universal here also, and to uphold the entire body of the truth, presenting it in its entirety, even though the priest who is called upon to fulfil that office of presenting it to the people may himself be actually living by the slenderest portion of it. No doubt we shall present most forcibly that part of the whole truth which is most real to ourselves; and for that reason, if no other, we ought to try our utmost to gain a personal apprehension of the whole. But men's spiritual diseases are of many kinds, and all the healing truths must be offered by the Church in which all men are to find life.

[#] This is a description of Sectarianism, not of any particular Denomination. We are all infected with the sectarian spirit. In many respects Rome is far more sectarian than the great Presbyterian bodies in Scotland. With all its faults I sincerely believe that the Anglican Communion is, in spirit, more of a Church and less of a sect than any other body. But then it contains several sects within itself, both "High," "Broad," and "Low."

The truth which it thus presents, the Church believes to be the gift of God. This above all is the idea which it tries to safeguard by the outward signs of regular orders and sacraments.

Our belief about the communion service is that there Christ comes to us just as once the eternal Word, which was present with all His creation, none the less came in full manifestation under the limitations of time and space at a particular moment and in a particular country. So in the communion the Divine presence which fills the whole world ("Heaven and earth are full of His glory," as we say in the service itself) is offered to us, and draws near to us; and that not because of any virtue in us; it was while we were yet sinners that Christ came and died; it is while we are yet sinners that Christ offers Himself to us; and it is as guarding against any conception that we can determine how He shall come, or when and where, and that we can, as it were, manufacture

His presence in our own way, that the Church maintains with the utmost emphasis the order that is necessary for that service.

It is to preserve the conception of spiritual life as a gift of God, and of the Church as the society which recognises and receives it as such a gift, in distinction from a mutual benefit society organised for the edification of its own members, that the Church insists upon the due order of its administration; and it is through concentration upon this idea of holiness, and all that it ought to mean in our personal lives, that we can make our greatest contribution towards bringing into existence again a real Catholic Church, a Church which shall genuinely include all the persons who believe in Christ in one order and fellowship. The first and indispensable condition of re-union is fuller dedication to the will of God in Christ. We shall be united to one another when we are all truly united to Him.

But, if that work is to be accomplished, we shall also need wisdom, in order rightly to counteract the effects alike of folly and of sin in the past history of the Church; and here every man must be willing to make what suggestions he can, merely submitting them for acceptance or rejection by the whole body of the Church; because unless people are prepared to speak of the problem as they see it, leaving the final judgment to be formed by the body of which they are members, there is no hope of our making any progress at all.

I will therefore, venture to suggest to you six principles, upon which, as my vision is at present, I think we might come near to agreement among ourselves; and if we should agree upon them, then we could offer these or whatever modifications of these the Church thinks fit, to those bodies which are at present in separation from us.

I.—First, what do we mean by the Church? Ideally and in its eternal reality it is the Body and Bride of Christ, the instrument of His will and the object of His love, worthy as both. But in the process of time and upon the stage of this world, what are we going to mean by it, and who are we going to account its members? When people begin to think of this question, they always start with various enthusiastic schemes. The members of the Church are the people who have faith, or the people who are conscious of the need of pardon, and the like; but all of this breaks down because you can never tell who these people are. We must have some perfectly plain outward sign if the Church is to be an operative agency in this world; and you will find, I think, that there is none which you can reach except that it is the fellowship of the baptized. Baptism is the Lord's own appointed way by which men should be received in the fellowship of His disciples. We must take that as our basis.

It is no business of ours to pronounce judgment upon the spiritual state of other persons. We shall thank God for every sign of the Christian virtues and graces shown in other persons who have not been brought to baptism; we may believe that they are members of the Church in heaven; but still, I would submit, we must say for all purposes of practical working, that the Church on earth is the fellowship of the baptized.

II.—That fellowship exists in fragments and sections. What is the peculiar mark of our fragment? This is authoritatively defined for us in the Lambeth Quadrilateral,[#] but our special character may be expressed briefly by saying that we are trustees for the Catholic order, who yet reject what seem to us the accretions which the Church of Rome upholds.

[#] (a) The Holy Scriptures of the Old and New Testaments. as "containing all things necessary to Salvation," and as being the rule and ultimate standard of faith.

(b) The Apostles' Creed, as the Baptismal Symbol; and the Nicene Creed, as the sufficient statement of the Christian faith.

(c) The two Sacraments ordained by Christ Himself—Baptism and the Supper of the Lord—ministered with unfailing use of Christ's words of institution, and of the elements ordained by Him.

(d) The Historic Episcopate, locally adapted in the methods of its administration to the varying needs of the nations and peoples called of God into the Unity of His Church.

Now some such order as that which we maintain, is necessary, as it seems to me, to the fulfilment of the duty of charity. I hope I am not unfair to those who are separated from us, and are influenced by the ideals of Puritanism; but it has seemed to me that their discipline is not always charitable. Indeed, a Church must either excommunicate freely or else possess a recognised order if it is to avoid becoming indistinguishable from "the world" about it; if it is to be both holy and a friend of sinners it must have an order. The order which we maintain is simply that which has come down to us as the actual order of historic Christendom.

III.—Thirdly, I would submit that the Body with its orders is a living whole, and that it is illegitimate to discuss such a question as the "validity" of Orders out of all relation to the historic life of the Church. The question of Orders must be considered in relation to the whole life of the Body of which they are an organic part.[#]

[#] See . On Orders and Catholicity.

Thus, if we take the famous Quadrilateral as our starting point, a body which stands by the Canonical Scriptures, the Creeds and the two great Sacraments, though not upholding the episcopal succession, is closer to the ideal than one which is indifferent to any of these three as well as to the succession; it has maintained many of the (ex hypothesi) essential features of a true Church; it approximates to the complete requirement. Moreover, within the field of the problem of Orders, there are degrees of approximation; it is generally considered that an agreement between the Anglican and Presbyterian communions could be far more easily reached than between the Anglican and some other Protestant bodies. We must, therefore, avoid two kindred errors. One is to set up the abrupt dilemma—"Either a true Church or not," and the other is to regard the possession of "valid" Orders as being the one and only condition of the Catholicity of the body possessing them.

The Church Visible cannot be identical with the Church Invisible; it is its sacrament. And the question resolves itself into one concerning the degree of adequacy with which it expresses, and thereby maintains through the ages, the fulness of the truth.

Our actual divisions in the West date from the Reformation. No one disputes that the Church just before that time was corrupt to a horrible degree. It is possible to hold that the corruption could have been purged away without schism if the reformers had been wholly free from pride and impatience; I see no means of reaching a sound judgment on such a point; but at least it would seem that the guilt for the great division was as much in Catholics as in Protestants. In so far as there really was necessity of choosing between moral purity with schism on the one hand, and organic unity with sales of indulgences and the like on the other, there can be no doubt which the whole teaching of Christ required His followers to choose. "I will have mercy and not sacrifice"; "the Sabbath was made for man, not man for the Sabbath"; yet the Sabbath and the sacrifice were of Divine appointment.

If then a fragment of the Church, confronted as it believes, with such a choice, breaks off and organises itself afresh, intending to maintain in purity all the Church's life and means of grace, I cannot assert that it is for all its generations deprived of Christ's sacramental presence. But assuredly the loss of the continuous order which so impressively symbolises the Divine origin of the Church and of its Sacraments tends to undermine the intention to preserve the whole truth and to obscure belief in it. For Orders, as we understand them, are the pledge of the unity of the Church across all space and through all time, so that the priest who celebrates, does so as the organ and instrument of the universal Church, and the congregation at every Eucharist is not the few persons gathered together in that building, but Angels and Archangels and all the company of Heaven, with whom we join in prayer and worship.

IV.—Consonantly with this I would come to my fourth principle—that the whole question of Orders and Sacraments must be considered in reference to the Church's life through the ages, and not with direct reference to the gift received by any individual at any given service.

How are we to secure (this is our problem) that from generation to generation men shall continue to feel that in the service of the Holy Communion Christ comes to them as by His own appointment, and they have only to be ready to meet with Him; and that in meeting with Him they are united with the whole Church in the Holy Communion, the Communion of Saints? I believe that the continued recitation of the Creeds in our own and other branches of the Church is the main safeguard, not only for ourselves but also for those who do not say the Creeds, against that combination of Pelagianism and Unitarianism to which men always tend to drift; similarly I can conceive that, just because we uphold the full conception of sacramental worship, others are enabled to receive sacramental grace at their communions. It may be so; I know not. Of course it cannot be received if it is not there; but even if it is there, its full benefit will not be enjoyed except by those who believe in its full power. Two men may stand opposite the same picture; both see the same lines and colours, the accidents; but it may be that only one sees the artistic reality or substance—the Beauty—while the other is blind to it. But the man who finds it does not put it there; the artist put it there; and if he had not done so no one could find it there; so too the reality of the Sacrament is the work of God. But our fruition of it depends on our faith, and even on the exact content of our faith. Now I do not for a moment believe that that faith in the full doctrine of sacramental grace can survive through the centuries, if it is once separated from the whole order which expresses it. Therefore, while I am not entitled to deny, as I am equally not concerned to assert, that the members of other denominations at their communion service receive the same gift that we do; still I say that as trustees for the Catholic order, and considering the matter in the light of the centuries, we have no right to sacrifice any of those means by which this full doctrine has been given to us, and by which perhaps it has been also preserved for them.

V.—Fifthly, I would suggest that in any scheme for practical reunion no man must be required to repudiate his own spiritual ancestry.

After all, if the Church is the fellowship of the baptized, then our brethren of the separation, as we sometimes call them, are members of the Church; but they are not members of our branch of the Church; and their faith is corporate and active in their membership of their own bodies; consequently we are bound to hold that they and their bodies are parts of the Catholic Church in this time of the division—the division which is due to sin.

If it is true that it was largely, and perhaps mainly, the fault of the medieval Church that the split became a necessity; if it is true that it was partly, and perhaps mainly, the fault of the Church of England that the Wesleyan movement (for example) ever broke off, because we refused to make room for what was in its early stages most undoubtedly a movement of the Spirit of God in the world, then we have no right to condemn those who by reason of our sin, at least as much as their own, are outside our fellowship; and we must recognise that, just as in St. Paul's argument about the true Israel, blindness in part happened to Israel, and so God used the Gentiles to provoke them to jealousy—so blindness in part happened to Catholicism, and God is using the Protestant bodies to provoke us to jealousy.

We must, I believe, maintain that our order is for us the only possible order for the reunited Church. But order is not everything. The wall of the Holy City is minute. When the time for reunion comes, we must insist upon our own part of the truth in such a way as to avoid all condemnation of other bodies for having been separated during this time—at least, all condemnation which we do not pronounce quite equally upon ourselves. What has happened in the divisions of the Church is a severance from one another of elements which are every one of them necessary to the healthy life of the Body. If one set of people could only get dry food and no drink, and another set could only get drink and no food, neither would be healthy. They would have to combine their stores before health was possible. Catholics have preserved perhaps a fuller sense of worship and of the gifts of God; Protestants have perhaps a truer zeal for righteousness and a more intimate access to God in prayer. Let us not judge the past; God will judge. But let us recognise our need of one another and accept from each other the positive truth and life which God has given to either.

VI.—Meanwhile, in the time of the division, different bodies have developed different types of religious life. There is a wealth of spiritual activity in the world now such as it is difficult to imagine under a rigidly united Church; but we can easily preserve that if we are ready that there should be within the United Catholic Church different Orders—an Order of St. George Fox for example, testifying to the great ideal which Christ brought into the world, not as I think, and as I have already explained, the right ideal to be followed by all men in all sorts of circumstances, but undoubtedly the one method by which in the end the work of God can be finally accomplished, and for testimony to which I believe some men, and indeed the whole Society of Friends, are even now called by God. Also there may well be an Order of St. John Wesley, insisting more especially upon the need of individual conversion, which the Church, as a vast organisation concerned with world movements, is perpetually tempted to leave too much on one side. These Orders can quite well govern themselves to a very large extent, and order their worship in very many ways, just as is the case in the Orders familiar in the medieval Church, and in the Church of Rome at this time.

These are the principles which I would venture to submit. Probably not one of them will win universal assent even in our own communion. But amid all our amiable sentiments it is time for somebody to say something definite, or as definite as the complexity of the problem allows. In criticising and rejecting individual utterances we may at last reach a corporate mind.

But let me add one particular warning about the way we go: for in my own mind I am quite sure that the Communion is just the place where we need to be divided until our unity is real. People say "How terrible to be separated there." Yes, terrible indeed! It is the measure of the sin of schism. But we must not try to escape the consequences of the sin until we have got rid of the sin itself. I say nothing of the problem of the mission field or of the possibility of exceptional occasions.[#] But I am quite sure that in normal Church life, where all people have access to their own services, intercommunion can only be disastrous, as tending to obscure the need for real unity, and the difference between the various excellences whose combination is to be desired.

[#] It must of course be recognised that the problem of intercommunion in the mission field is of urgent practical importance. On the present situation, the Archbishop of Canterbury's statement, Kikuyu.

But let us come back to what after all is the only true guarantee and the only condition of reunion—the achievement of holiness; that holiness needs, as we have seen, to be safeguarded, and the safeguarding of it is peculiarly entrusted to us, the ministers of the Church. What need then for personal dedication! For upon the degree in which we are wholly given to our work depends in large measure the time when God will reunite His Church.

We keep separate even from many right activities, but only in order to keep pure that spirit by which we are to permeate the whole life of the world, bringing it to bear, so far as we are able in our detachment, upon every sort of problem, private or public—industrial, commercial, political, international—till at last the whole world is governed by that spirit, and there is no need for separation any more nor for any special place of worship nor special order of religious ministers; for then the world and the Church will be indistinguishable in the Holy City of God, wherein is no temple, because the Lord God Almighty and the Lamb are the temple of it.

LECTURE V

THE CITIZENSHIP OF HEAVEN

"Our citizenship is in heaven."—Philippians iii. 20.

"He that hath seen me hath seen the Father."—S. John xiv. 9.

We have considered in outline the functions of the State and of the Church, the two great instruments of God for the furthering of His kingdom. Let us now turn to consider, still in mere outline, for nothing more is possible, the nature of that Kingdom itself.

There are very many ways in which the subject might be approached, but I think that it will be most consonant with the general line of our thought in these meditations that we should consider it as the home of man's spirit, the fulfilment of his spiritual being. And to that end, inasmuch as the Kingdom can only be known by living according to the principles of its citizenship, and our present effort is by its very nature intellectual only, we must try to reach it in thought as the goal towards which the whole spiritual life of man is tending.

No life can be set forth in scientific terms. The moment it is analysed, the vitalising power is gone. And even the poet, who has far more chance than the logician of making us realise what the life signifies for those who live it, is still speaking of it from outside. It is only by life itself that we can truly know the Kingdom of God.

We find, all through the New Testament, a contrast drawn between earth and heaven. And it is worth while to consider the logical principle of that contrast, even though the result is somewhat dry and barren. The place of careful analysis here is analogous to that which criticism holds in relation to art. The critical analysis of a work of art will never of itself enable us to appreciate it, if we are without the cultivated artistic faculty; but it may enrich our appreciation. We may thereby find more than we should otherwise have found of the elements that are combined together to make up the total effect. And then in the unity of the renewed experience we receive more enjoyment than we had done before. So, too, the Kingdom of God, which for us is something that we still hope to reach, and of which the foretaste that we have as yet received is a very slight earnest of the glory that shall be revealed, may be a goal more potent in its attraction to our wills, when we have seen it as the fulfilment of the principles of our whole spiritual life as these are discoverable in other departments and activities.

The goods of this world, as we have already noticed, are such that the more one has the less there is for others. The goods of heaven are of such a kind that the more one has the more there is on that account for others. So it is with the true virtues of the spiritual life, with love and joy and peace, the fruits of the spirit. So it is too with other excellences which belong to man as a spiritual being, and which are out of the reach of our animal nature: loyalty, beauty and knowledge.

Now the principle of this whole spiritual life is precisely the principle of unity, not as distinct from variety but as distinct either from antagonism or transitoriness. The two things that distress the soul of man are enmities, and the passing away of that which he loves. It is by rising above these evils, which beset us in this earthly state, that the satisfaction of the soul is found.

There are four main departments of the spiritual life which aspire in this way to rise above the evils which beset our mortal state. They are Science and Art and Morality and Religion. As we know them in our experience, they are all of them due on the human side to a dissatisfaction with our experience as we find it. The scientific man is disturbed by the apparent chaos in his experience, and he sets out to give order to it, and he is satisfied in so far as he discovers that all the while it was not chaotic, as it seemed, but orderly. The artist is craving for a beauty which, in his ordinary experience, he does not find. He selects, he concentrates attention on certain aspects, to reach a satisfaction which the world otherwise seems not to give. The man of moral aspiration is dissatisfied with the world as he sees it, and he sets himself therefore to alter both himself and it, that it may be modelled more in accordance with the heart's desire. And the religious man finds all of these sources of dissatisfaction working together within his soul; he seeks, and in faith finds, that which gives him both peace and power.

Let us then begin with what is in itself the least rich of these forms of human activity, and consider how it is that Science reaches its unity. Let us first recall that there are two forms of multiplicity or division which we are seeking to overcome: that which arises from the clash of various ideals or desires, the antagonism of man with man; and that which arises from the changeableness of the world as we see it. With regard to the latter, science does indeed reach real unities; but they are unities which leave Time out of sight. Sometimes, no doubt, the subject matter which is handled is itself non-temporal, but not in the sense of being eternal. So, for example, geometry is entirely without relation to time. There is no temporal sequence between the equality of the sides and the equality of the angles in the isosceles triangle. But where the subject studied is something that changes in Time, it remains true that the aim of science is to reach an unchanging principle. So, for example, the student of biology may be trying to discover the unchanging principle which governs the successive variations of species. But when he has found it he has not really mastered the transitoriness; he has not in any way gathered up the past and dead into his present experience; he has merely found the principle which applies to every stage as that stage comes. He reaches some superiority to the transitoriness of things, only by abstracting from Time altogether.

And, similarly, the unity between men which is produced by a common absorption in such pursuits does not strike very deep. For a man's temperament has nothing in the world to do with his scientific conclusions, or at least ought not to have. In the ideal pursuit of knowledge, all of the things that set men at variance count for nothing whatever. Consequently the differences, just because they are ignored, are not overcome, with the result that, as at the beginning of this war, we may find professors of the various nations, who had been linked together, as one might think, closely enough in the pursuit of knowledge, hurling manifestoes at one another across their national frontiers.

When we pass to the second of the great departments, a real progress may be noted in just these points. For in the experience of the artist Time is genuinely mastered. We get some illustration of this from the absorption which marks the aesthetic contemplation of a picture or a statue. For the time that we are really held by it, we forget about time altogether. But the case is clearer with regard to those arts which handle temporal processes—music and poetry. For it is the whole point, let us say, of a drama, that it shall follow a certain succession; it is vital to its significance that the scenes shall be in that order and no other. If you have two plays, each in three acts, in one of which the first act is cheerful in tone, and the second is neutral, and the third depressing, while in the other the first act is depressing, the second neutral, and the third cheerful, the total effect of the two plays is not the average of the three acts in each case, which would be neutral for both, but is in the one particularly depressing, and in the other particularly cheering. For the play is grasped as a whole. It makes a single impression, if it is a good play. We know what it means—not indeed because we can state it in other words, for it is the only expression of its own meaning; but it has a definite significance for us. And the name of the play comes to stand for that significance. This is especially noticeable in tragedy, where the Greeks, with their sure instinct, chose a story whose plot is known to the spectator in advance, so that we have throughout the play both the impression of the entire story and the particular impression of each scene as it comes and passes. It is significant that the Greeks did so choose for tragedy stories whose plot was known, while their comedians invented their own plots. And most will agree that we enjoy a great play better when we have read it in advance, or when we have already seen it on the stage before; because then we do reach something that may serve perhaps as the nearest image that we can get for eternity—a grasp of the whole stretch of time, realised in its successiveness and in the meaning which that successiveness gives to it, and having the sense of the whole throughout and seeing each moment, as it comes, in the light not only of the past but of the future too.

On this side, then, art is able, for the moment at least, and with regard to a period definitely limited by our capacities of comprehension, to master Time and give us a unity which includes its successiveness within it; so that the past, and even the future, are gathered up into the real experience of the present, and we are not only conscious of what is before our eyes, but are conscious of it as a part of the whole to which it belongs.

In a similar way we notice that while different temperaments are needed for the production of different types of art, yet in appreciation all are united. For example, it would be quite impossible for the great Russian novels to be produced in any other country than Russia; it would have been quite impossible for the great German philosophy to have been produced in any other nation than Germany; it would have been quite impossible for the great English poetry to have been produced in any other nation than England. These literatures belong to the soil out of which they spring. But the people of all the other nations can appreciate them, and all are glad because they are different. And so far as the artistic side of our nature governs our whole being, it is capable of linking us together in a real fellowship, which includes and is based upon our differences and the appreciation of them, and is therefore firmly rooted, because what might have been the source of antagonism is become itself the bond of unity.

But we must notice that each of these only reaches a very provisional attainment. If science likes to mark off a certain department of reality for its investigation, it can reach something like finality concerning just that department. I suppose that mechanics is something like a complete system of truth, so far as the mechanical aspect of things can be isolated from all other aspects. But then, nothing in the world is mechanical and only mechanical. Nothing in the world is chemical and only chemical. There are always other qualities there, from which abstraction has been made. Science therefore inevitably sets before itself as its goal the understanding of the universe, and it could not reach any absolute certainty concerning any real fact except so far as it had obtained omniscience. In mathematics it reaches certainty, because in mathematics the object is what it is defined to be, and nothing else. But no given material thing is just a triangle. It may even be disputed whether any given thing can be, according to the definition, a triangle at all.

Science then is marked by a restlessness until it reaches this omniscience. It began when the first man said "Why?" The moment that question is asked, Science is launched upon its course. But the answer to that question merely prompts anyone of scientific instincts to say "Why?" to the answer. Why is there a war? Historical science will point to the diplomatic documents, and from them to the course of history moulding national aspiration. Then if we say, "Why was the cause of war such? And, why were there such national aspirations?" we shall find ourselves soon investigating the literature of the countries and then their climates; from this we are shortly involved in astronomy and geology and all the other sciences. You can have nothing that is final until you reach omniscience. And so Science moves, perpetually saying "Why?" to every statement that is made. Far in the distance, in the infinite distance, is its goal of a complete satisfaction gained through understanding the universe in its entirety.

Art can similarly only achieve a provisional attainment of its goal; but the attainment while it lasts is more substantial. Its method, as distinct from that of science, is mental rest. The aim of the artist is to concentrate attention upon the object, holding it there by various devices. That is why pictures are put into frames. Something abruptly irrelevant, although not discordant, is put round the object to help us fix our minds upon it. That is why poetry is written in metre. The mind is abruptly brought back by the recurrence of the rhythm or the recurrence of the sound in rhyme, and held within the total composition. We notice that it is precisely where the subject matter of the poem is slight that the rhythm needs to be strongly marked or the system of rhyme complicated; where the subject matter itself has a strong appeal, any rhyming seems to be out of place and tiresome. The aim is simply to grip the attention and hold it upon the object and make us see it as it is; not after the fashion of science, connecting it with other things, but understanding it by getting to know it in and for itself as thoroughly as may be.[#] Now in thus concentrating attention upon some one object and claiming complete absorption in that object, art is implicitly claiming to give a perfect mental satisfaction and an absolute peace. But it can never succeed in that unless the object upon which it is concentrating our attention is an adequate symbol for the whole truth of things in which the whole of our nature will find such satisfaction.

[#] This is why no great work of art over becomes out of date, whereas the work of a great scientist is always liable to do so, because his successors revise it in the light of ever widening knowledge.

Moreover, these activities of the mind or spirit fail to govern our lives as a whole precisely because they are contemplative and not active. We stand before the world gazing at it, setting our minds indeed to work upon it in certain ways, yet not fundamentally changing it. But we are active beings, with wills as well as contemplative minds, and our volitional action lies very largely outside the range which these activities and interests can control. And therefore it is that so little real unity is reached by means of them.

In Morality the practical instincts and impulses are for the first time included. Morality is the science or the art, or both, of living in society; of living, that is to say, as fellow members with other beings, who also have aspirations and ideals as legitimate as our own, so that our own claim to pursue our own ideals must be won by recognition of their equal claim to pursue theirs.

And the man who, with full mastery of himself, if such a man exists, is following out a great purpose that is adequate to satisfy his whole nature, is a man who has achieved the conquest of Time in the completest way. It is essential to the pursuit of a purpose that we move from stage to stage, as we adapt means to our end, and yet all of it is one thing, thought and experienced as one. Indeed a test that we always instinctively apply to a biography is whether it enables us to see the different stages of a man's life as constituting one spiritual whole. That is just what we desire the biographer to set forth before us.

At the same time Morality conquers antagonism because it is the life of fellowship. It begins with the recognition that other men have as much right to live as we have, and we buy our rights precisely by conceding theirs. Its root principle is the recognition of this brotherhood or fellow-membership. And yet it, too, never reaches its goal; it fails in two ways; every man in this world, however perfectly he may achieve mastery of his own nature—and it may be doubted if any man has ever done even that by his own strength—is so conditioned by circumstances that he is never able to make his life a perfect masterpiece of art; and as regards the whole fellowship of which he is a member, and his own relation to it, he can find no absolute rules except the command to reach a state of mind which he cannot reach by his own will. There are no moral laws that are absolute except the law to love one's neighbour as oneself. All the rest have exceptions somewhere. "Thou shall not kill," was the formula of the old law. But we have altered it into, "Thou shalt do no murder." It is always wrong to murder, because murder is such killing as is wrong. But it is not always wrong to kill. And so we find no principle that can be made entirely binding and universal, except the law to love our neighbour as ourselves. But how are we to do it? Is there any man who seriously thinks that by taking thought he can make himself love somebody else?

All of these three then, and the last as emphatically as any, in spite of its comprehending a greater section of human nature, fail to reach their own achievement.

In the fourth stage, in Religion, all would find their fulfilment. For the purpose of God, if there be a God, is the principle of unity which the scientist is seeking. The nature of God, if there be a God, is that perfect beauty which would be the culmination of the life of Art. The righteousness of God, if there be a God, is the satisfaction of the moral aspiration. But we are not left so to conjecture what life would be like if we could carry our own spiritual faculties to their own highest development. We are given the express image of the person of God. "He that hath seen Me hath seen the Father." We shall not indeed have perfect knowledge of the sphere of religion until we have seen how the whole of history and every detail of our lives is, after all, the result and work of creative Love; but while Science and Art and Morality struggle towards their goal and only realise their need for it, God gives Himself as the satisfaction of that need. It is His gift, not our discovery; but we see that in this principle all Time is gathered up, for if the life of Christ is the manifestation of the nature of God, then it is the manifestation of the root-principle of all history.[#]

[#] I am aware that the argument here is per saltum, but space forbids its full development. I hope soon to have completed a book which will fill in the outline sketch offered in this Lecture.

Meanwhile I would refer to my essay on The Divinity of Christ in Foundations, specially pp. 213-223, 242-263.

Then we see, too, how all men may be united in perfect fellowship, because all men loving God will find themselves loving those whom God so loves. This hope or conviction remains in the region of faith, not of knowledge; what of that? In the other departments also we have found no knowledge. We have only found approximation towards it. We have, as it were, converging lines which never meet; and we have also the point at which we see they would meet if produced. Is that not enough? Here we find is the principle that will give unity, as we work it out, to the whole scheme of our spiritual life. Morality says, "Love all men." How can I? Science says, "Realise the truth which explains the universe." How can I? But I can gaze upon the manifestation of God in Jesus Christ; I can meditate upon His Cross and Resurrection. I can see here and there how it may be true that this is indeed the explanation of all the sorrow, even of all the sin. For if it is true that the supreme manifestation of the love of God was historically conditioned by the supreme sin of humanity in the treason of Judas, then surely one begins to see how even out of the grossest evil the glory of God wins triumph for itself, which we too may share if we are first drawn to share the sacrifice.

As I become absorbed in that contemplation I find in the first place a new power to love all men, as I remember that He died for them just as He died for me. In the degree in which I really believe that this is the manifestation of the power of God and the governing authority of the universe, I find this thought over-ruling other thoughts and temptations to hostility or enmity. As I remember that those whom I am inclined to despise or hate are those for whom He thought it worth while to die, my contempt and my hatred are rebuked and cancelled.

And similarly, if I realise—or in the degree in which I realise—that here is set forth the power that governs all things, that this is the way in which God rules the world, and that Calvary is the mode of His omnipotence, I begin to find myself indifferent, and that increasingly, to those things which are called sorrow and pain.

But we shall only find this as we expect to find it. All through our spiritual life we may be perpetually in contact, as it were, with the means of receiving what is good, and never receive it because we are not expecting it. We have not expected peace of mind from our worship, we have not expected a sense of security against evil; that is why we have not found it; but it is our fault. And certainly most of us have not expected to find fellowship from worship. We have known something of the grace of Jesus Christ, perhaps even of the love of God; but of the fellowship of the Holy Spirit, of the sense of being linked to one another because all dominated by that one power, most of us have found nothing, because we have not expected it.

But if we are expecting this, all the testimony of the saints in every generation goes to show that we shall find what we have expected.

The power that can give us security against the transitoriness of the world and against the instincts of antagonism is there in the faith that we place in God. "I will put my trust in God," the Psalmist says, "I will not fear what flesh can do unto me." This is not because flesh will not do such hurt as it can to the man who puts his trust in God—the Jews crucified Christ—but because to the man who puts his trust in God, anything whatever that happens becomes part of God's purpose for his life, and therefore he will not fear it. For "all things," sorrow as well as joy, pain as well as pleasure, sin as well as righteousness, "all things work together for good to them that love God."

LECTURE VI

GOD IN HISTORY

"I am the Alpha and the Omega, saith the Lord God, which is and which was and which is to come, the Almighty."—Revelation i. 8.

We have considered the two great instruments of God by which He fashions the spiritual life of man, and we have considered that spiritual life itself in the outline at least of its four main departments; and now, as we close our line of thought, we need still to consider how it is that, in these fields and by these instruments, God carries forward His work.

The conception of God as at work in human history, guiding it, controlling it, and judging men by its course, is the great contribution of Israel to the religion of the world. It is linked of course with that belief in the union of perfect righteousness with the divine, power which we usually speak of under the somewhat cumbrous title of Ethical Monotheism. We remember what was really at stake in that great day upon Mount Carmel when Elijah confronted the priests of Baal; it was whether the conception of God as righteous and demanding righteousness should prevail, or the conception of God as a capricious Being, needing only to be propitiated, and in connection with whose very worship licentiousness was tolerated and even encouraged.

But, after all, the greatest souls, at least in every highly-developed religion, have believed that God is righteous in Himself. What gives to Israel its supreme significance in the spiritual history of mankind is the conviction that this righteous God is daily and hourly at work in the history of men; and that conviction gives to the faith of Israel a primacy and supremacy over all the other partial faiths, even though they may be superior in certain departments.

If we think of some of the conceptions by means of which we try to bring before our minds the meaning of the word "God," we may find that with regard to several of them, other nations had advanced further than Israel before the coming of the Lord.

God is Spirit. The Hindu knew that, and knows it still, quite as much as Israel.

God is Law. The more thoughtful at least among the ancient Romans, and particularly the great Roman Stoics, knew that with a vividness that was scarcely ever attained in Israel.

God is Beauty. Assuredly the ancient Greeks knew that as Israel never realised it at all.

But the conception of Israel that God is at work in history means that the God of Israel gives to these other gods or conceptions of God, each its own time and place of emergence and decay. The God who is revealed to us in the Old Testament is Himself the Being who appoints that the Indian or the Roman or the Greek should reach these particular convictions; and in these partial apprehensions of the Divine, before the full revelation came, the faith of Israel is determinative and regulative for all the other faiths; and moreover, it is this faith that God is at work in the actual daily history of men, which makes the faith of Israel the natural and proper introduction to the Incarnation, where God Himself took flesh and lived among men and died at a time and in a place—in Palestine and under Pontius Pilate.

This exaltation of the Holy God, actually at work within men and at their side, while it leads to a sense of awe before the Holiness of the Almighty, also leads to a sense of the dignity of this world, and of man's life in it, which is lacking, as a rule, from other great religions, and that too in proportion as those other religions are spiritual. For the Hindu, for example, this world and all that is in it is mere illusion. He is spiritual enough but he is not material enough; and we find there that contempt for the things of the body which invariably issues in a contempt for moral conduct; for our moral conduct here, while we live upon this planet, is wrought out through our bodies. But the religion of Israel, and especially its completion in the Incarnation, wherein God Himself came in the flesh, gives at once a dignity to this world of ours, to our bodies, and to all the material side of life.

When Christ stood before Pilate, the Kingdom of God was in appearance, at least, undergoing judgment at the hands of the kingdom of this world; but it is not merely a contrast of good with evil. It is a contrast of the perfect with the very imperfect, but yet not merely evil, power. Pilate is not Satan; and the Lord Himself, in the moment of His trial, recognises that the authority by which He is condemned is an authority that is derived from God—"Thou couldest have no power at all against Me, except it were given thee from above." The kingdoms of this world, which are to become the kingdoms of our God and of His Christ, are not simply something evil. The contrast of Church and World is not the contrast between good and evil; but it is the contrast between two stages in the work which God is accomplishing in history, and those two may often come into conflict.

Let us then ask what is the central principle of God's guidance of His people, so far as it may be deduced from the tiny fragment of history that we really know. In that fragment at least, we may say, I think, with little hesitation, that its method and its aim is spiritual growth, or, if you like to put it an expansion and enrichment of personality.

We are sometimes inclined to think our own personality is something that is given to us from the outset, and entirely belongs to us; but that idea will not stand examination for a moment. Individual personality is a social product. It can only be developed under social influences. A man may be born with many great talents, but if his environment does not encourage their development, these talents will remain for the most part undeveloped and unknown—either to himself or to anybody else. Indeed the greater the talent with which a man is endowed, the more difference is made to him by the kind of surroundings in which he is put. A man of very few gifts and little natural capacity will be much the same, whether he has abundant opportunity for mental and spiritual growth or little opportunity; but the man of great capacities, needing for their development the encouragement of surroundings, is an entirely different being according as those surroundings are favourable or the reverse; and so we reach the curious result that the greatest personality, while no doubt he must have brought into the world something given to him by God that was capable of development, is yet more entirely dependent upon the society in which he is living than people with a less wide range of gifts.

Again, it is only within a society which has developed some character for itself, which has indeed a personality of its own, that individual personality can reach very much development. You cannot have genius in a savage tribe. Genius is the focal expression of the personality of a whole people. It is that people coming to life, and possessed of voice; and you do not find it where there is little social development. It is only as the tribe or the nation begins to have some definite character of its own that it is itself sufficiently organised to develop from its own individual member those gifts, and elicit those activities, which are the signs of genius.

We find then, that individual personality, or spiritual life, is dependent upon the spiritual life of society; and we need to notice that this society has every mark by which we distinguish personality in the individual. It has aspirations: it has a predominant character; it has claims, and it has duties. It has in fact, in the literal sense of the word, corporate personality, and just as the many instincts and impulses which are to be found in human nature, and may be very discordant with one another, are welded together to make up the single life of a human being, so the whole gifts and instincts and ambitions and aspirations of all the individual citizens are welded together, to make up the personality of the whole society.

Moreover, every nation is in itself not only the combination of individual citizens, but also of minor groups within itself, all of which have these same marks, and all of which are in the real genuine sense persons, spiritual individuals with a life of their own.

Now, as we look over the history of the development which thus goes on side by side in the individual and in society, we find that its principle in the fragment of history that we really know has been that isolated excellences should be brought to perfection first; and after something like perfection has been reached in the separate departments taken singly, the combination of them is brought about, in order that the richer and fuller life may be perfected, in which all of them find a place.

European history derives its whole life from Palestine, Greece and Rome; and in each of those three peoples, some one excellence was developed to a peculiar degree. Rome perfected and has bequeathed to us the instincts for social order, as embodied in law. The history of the Roman people is of significance, precisely because one may there trace the growth and working out of this instinct for social or political life. There has never been anything to rival it in history. No modern nation has shown the same extraordinary political sense and sanity. The Romans were not great political philosophers. They did not think very much about the principles on which they acted; but simply because of their peculiar gift in this direction they welded together a social order which lasted throughout their Empire in a wonderful way; and to this day the law of Europe is to an enormous extent the law of ancient Rome.

To ancient Greece, it is hard to say what we do not owe. Her peculiar characteristic is intellectual passion; a passion for reaching perfection in just what the intellect is particularly qualified to grasp, truth and beauty. No doubt the ancient Greeks themselves thought a great deal about their ordinary politics and their military activities, and the wars between the various States; but these matter very little. The Greek people are significant for evermore not because of the Athenian trireme or the Macedonian phalanx, but because Aeschylus stood in astonished awe before the operation of the Divine Justice; because Sophocles reflected the whole of human life, even its ugliest manifestations, in the mirror of a soul so calm and pure, that as we look at that reflection all life seems bathed in peace and beauty; because Euripides entered into the sorrows of simple folk; because Thucydides, with a still unrivalled zeal for the genuine truth of history, said the wise word about nearly every political condition that has arisen since his time; because Plato dreamed "a Vision of all time and all existence," proclaimed that it can never be just to do harm to any man whatever harm he may have done to us; proclaimed also that "God is in no way unrighteous, but in all ways absolutely righteous, nor is anything more like to God than whosoever among men shall become perfectly righteous;" foreseeing also that if a perfectly righteous man should come on earth he would die, scourged and crucified.[#] There is nowhere before the New Testament anything that comes nearer to its own highest truths, not in the Old Testament itself, than what you will find in Plato.

[#] Republic i. 335*d*; Theaetetus 176*c*; Republic ii. 361*e*.

This influence,—the influence of this intellectual passion—has been the driving force in nearly all the movements since that time. It has been said there is nothing in the world which moves that is not Greek in origin, and it is almost true; it is from the Greeks that we have learnt "the use of reason to modify experience" and they derived it from the intellectual passion for truth and beauty.

To Palestine we owe the inspiring and governing faith of which I have already spoken—the one faith that can give real significance to these other two, faith in the Holy God at work in history.

It is noticeable that each of these countries was conspicuously weak in those other qualities which were not especially entrusted to it. Ancient Rome was not at all specially religious and was conspicuously unintellectual. The people of Greece again are not conspicuously religious, though in their cults there is a haunting beauty; and they were not at all politically successful; the history of Athens, the flower of Greece, is the history of a State in which almost every generation threw up a supreme genius who proceeded to change the constitution in accordance with his magnificent ideas; the result was political instability of an appalling character.[#] And Palestine has contributed very little to us as regards social organisation, and is markedly lacking in the scientific and artistic gifts. We have only to consider the great images that are set before us, let us say in the Book of Ezekiel, or again in the Book of Revelation, to see that there is no attempt in these efforts of the imagination to achieve a beautiful or harmonious whole. The symbolic elements are added one to another because of the value of their meaning; but there is no effort to visualise the whole; and if we try to make it, we quickly find that such a thing was never intended.

[#] It is of course true that the Greek genius gave us what we now mean by civilisation, namely, the combination of political unity and personal freedom. On this see the admirable first chapter of Mr. Edwyn Bevan's The House of Seleucus. But it remains true that the race from whose intellectual genius this whole product sprang had not in any considerable degree the capacity for controlling their own invention.

Each of these then reached a genuine supremacy in its own department; and the history of

Europe is to an enormous extent the history of the inter-action of these three forces as they mingle and combine in the polities of the barbarian invaders who wrecked the Roman Empire. We watch the periods of domination of each successively. Christianity grew up within the Roman Empire, and the fascination of that great Empire cast a glamour about it in the minds even of those who destroyed it, so that the life which emerges out of chaos in the Middle Ages is predominantly very Latin. The Renaissance is precisely the invasion of Greek influence, and the Reformation is very largely the rediscovery of the Hebrew.

For a while the three new forces worked together, carrying men's thought and action forward; and then in the 18th century it would seem that there was, in England at any rate, a torpor due to their exhaustion; when revival came it was because Wesley and his friends revived the Hebrew element in our life, because Newman and Pusey with their friends revived the Latin element, and because F. D. Maurice and the Broad Church movement revived the Hellenistic, and this, with its passion for more adequate comprehension and expression, is the dominant force of our time. We watch these three influences still at work; but as they interact upon one another and within the persons of the new races, a new product is gradually being produced, and in those corporate personalities which we call nations, we see a character being born which is something that history has not known before.

The first requirement of personality is always freedom—freedom as we have already said in its two senses, that conduct is not dictated from without but is governed by the whole person, and not by isolated elements; and the corporate persons need freedom just as much as the individual; hence the need, the vital and absolute need, for political sovereignty in any State which is conscious of itself as a person, that is as having a single spiritual life.

But that life and freedom are exercised only in the citizens who are members of the State. We cannot surely assert that the corporate person is immortal, as the individual is; and therefore, to destroy a State is to inflict a more irreparable loss than to kill a man, which is one reason at least, perhaps the chief reason, why a man should die for the political freedom of his country, and even, if need be, kill for it; but, as freedom is the first requirement of personality, fellowship is its first duty, for it is true of corporate personalities quite as much as of individuals that they only find themselves and fulfil themselves in their inter-action upon one another, and the nations of the world do in fact need one another, and need one another's full life.

In economics we found out long ago that in order to be wealthy, a country needs rich neighbours who may afford good markets. It is so in every other department. We need the gifts of the other peoples. We need that they shall be free and vigorous. Indeed the chief lesson which the world at this time needs to learn is just this—that all the nations of the world need one another, each needing also that the others should be free, in order that they may bring their contributions to the common life in which all share.

But we should, I think, be reading the signs of the times amiss if we did not also take account of the fact that there has been growing up lately a new type of corporate personality, not known to history before, and exemplified by your own United States and by the British Empire; the conception of sovereign States linked together in a single life, and exercising therein a joint sovereignty in dealing with those who lie outside the federation, is something of which history bears no record; and we need to try to understand its principle, and see what it is capable of contributing to the life of men in order that we may not fail to use our opportunity, and bring our contribution.[#]

[#] See . On Providence in History.

There is our outline sketch of the way in which the history of our own civilisation has grown, within which the Church and Nation are at work. We are members of both. What duty falls upon us as the result of that dual membership? The Christian citizen is called of necessity to fulfil one of three functions—prophet, priest and king.

The prophet is one who is called to testify to the ideal unflinchingly, not considering consequences, not perhaps considering ways and means of reaching the ideal, but simply insisting on its nature and calling men and nations to penitence so far as they fail to reach it. It may require more courage than the office of the king or statesman, and yet in itself it is the easiest, because it is relatively simple.

In all modern nations, and more so in the degree in which they are democratic, every citizen partakes of the duty of kingship. He has some share in determining how his nation shall act, either in the management of its own internal affairs or in its dealings with other people, and one who has this responsibility and is also a Christian, is involved in the absolute duty of trying to think, and to think with genuine effort, how he may be actually guiding his nation toward the ideal. He must not be content with pious platitudes leading to no action, nor content to consider only his own country's welfare; but as a member of the Church of Christ which embraces all mankind, he is called to think out and, having thought, to pursue in act the methods by which his nation may genuinely be doing its part to build up the one great Temple of God—His Holy City.

The priest is prophet and statesman, both at once. He, as minister of the Word of God, must perpetually insist upon the true ideal, and bid men to guard against all self-contentment so far as they fail to reach it; and yet he must be ready to take his stand by the side of every individual or group of individuals, even of the nation itself, nerving each to do the best of which it then and there in the circumstances of the day is capable. And meanwhile he is a wretched human being like the rest, terribly liable to pride if he upholds an ideal higher than is usually recognised; terribly liable to worldliness, alike in his own soul and in his teaching, if for a single moment he forsakes the Divine Presence; and uniquely exposed to the deadliest of all temptations; for while we preach what neither we nor anybody else can practise, we are sorely tempted to be content with spiritual mediocrity ourselves.

But above all, at this time the necessity, I think, is for a clear testimony concerning the purpose of God for His people, and His kingdom that shall surely come. We have made our precepts so tame; our efforts for peace and fellowship have been so much less exhilarating than other men's efforts for war; we have been very mild; and that is not the spirit of Christ, or of His Kingdom. The spirit of Christ is the spirit of all heroism in all ages.

In 1848, a little republic was founded in Rome to stand for justice and purity of government amid the corrupt States all round. It was attacked by those States, and at last it yielded; on the day when the capitulation was signed masses of people were gathered together in the great Piazza outside St. Peter's, and there rode among them the man whose faith and heroism had sustained that siege for more weeks than the wiseacres thought it could last days. When the cheering had subsided, he made no acknowledgment, but simply said:

And they streamed out after him into the hills. His name was Garibaldi; and because of his heroism and theirs the kingdom of Italy is in the world to-day.

But the invitation of Christ is in exactly that spirit—"I offer neither quarters, nor provisions, nor wages. I offer hunger, thirst, forced marches, battles, death." "If any man would come after Me, let him deny himself, and take up his cross, and follow Me."

The cross, when our Lord spoke those words, was quite a real thing. To take up the cross did not mean bearing life's little inconveniences with equanimity. It meant literally to put the rope round one's neck, and be ready simply for anything that might come. That is the spirit in which we are summoned to work for Christ. Can we rise to it? The Prince of Peace was not a "mild man." This is the vision that His disciple had of Him:

Can we present the figure of Christ as endowed with anything like that compelling power? If so, we are worthy ministers. It not, we are making dull the one great adventure of the world.

There is only one way in which we can succeed. It is that we cling to faith in God, the Author of the drama, in which we play our part; God, Himself the Guide along the path we are to follow; God, not only the Guide, but the very Way in which we are to walk; God, not only the Guide and Way, but the Strengthener within our souls, enabling us to follow; and God the Guide, the Way, the Strengthener, Himself also the Goal to which we would come. "For in Him we move and live and have our being."

I am the Alpha and the Omega, saith the Lord God, which is and which was and which is to come, the Almighty.

APPENDIX I

ON THE APOCALYPTIC CONSCIOUSNESS

It is very difficult for the modern reader to recover the frame of mind in which Apocalypse has its origin, but we may do this more easily if we look for parallels outside the field of religious history. It has been well said that the mediæval man looked upwards and downwards—to Hell and to Heaven; his view of the world is on a vertical plane; the modern man has a horizontal view, looking to the past and future—the past as it has existed, and the future as it shall exist, in the history of human society upon this earth. We need if possible to combine these two, but it is a very difficult achievement. With our point of view we inevitably read Apocalypse as if it were a literal history of the future written before the event; but this is not its primary significance. The religious consciousness from which it springs was highly indifferent to the lapse of time: very likely the seer expected the speedy realisation of his vision so far as he thought about things in that way at all, but this was not his primary concern. Let us take a parallel, as was suggested a moment ago, from another field. The socialistic movement in its early days seemed committed to an immediate expectation of the millennium following upon a catastrophic change in the structure of human society. The arrival of the millennium now seems postponed indefinitely and evolution has taken the place of revolution as a method, and yet a socialist who is really in the movement does not feel any breach of continuity; he knows that he is one in spirit with the earlier writers and that they were never mainly concerned either with the date at which the millennium would come or the means by which they imagined it brought about, but precisely with the contrast between the ideal as they conceived it and the actual as they saw it.

We may take another instance from a slightly different department of thought. Dante imagined that the Mount of Purgatory was the immediate antipodes of the Hill of Zion, but if some traveller had gone round the world and assured him that the Mount of Purgatory was not there, it would not in the smallest degree have affected his doctrine of Purgatory. So it is with the apocalyptists; there is an immense amount of machinery provided by which this world is to be abruptly changed into the Kingdom of God, and because that Kingdom is so present to the consciousness of the writer, he can speak of it as even now about to appear upon the earth. But this is not what chiefly interests him: his point of view is vertical, not horizontal; all time-spans are foreshortened into a moment, because his whole interest is in the contrast between the Kingdom of God and the kingdoms of this world; we therefore do him wrong in supposing that the postponement of his hope is any grievous disappointment, or any proof of real error. The date of its fulfilment was never a matter of much concern to him.

So we may, I think, reverently believe that our Lord Himself passes through the experience of the apocalyptists at moments of great exultation, as, for example, when the seventy return and say that the devils are made subject to them, or when He realises the imminence of the fall of Jerusalem, and therefore the removal of the chief barrier to His Kingdom's progress. All time is foreshortened; Satan falls from Heaven and the Son of Man appears in glory; but this is no forecast of history as we understand history. One evangelist tells us of a parable which He uttered precisely because of His perception that the disciples erroneously supposed "that the Kingdom of God was immediately to appear." All His insistence upon the coming Kingdom is focussed in the Passion, as has been shown in the text. When the revelation of God's inmost nature was completed in the completion of His own self-sacrifice, this brought with it the power that could change the kingdoms of this world into the Kingdom of our God and of His Christ. From then onwards "He cometh with the clouds"; but the completion of His Kingdom when "every eye shall see Him, and they which pierced Him," lies still in the future. The contrast of tenses in this passage can hardly be accidental; from the moment when He was lifted up from the earth in the Passion, Resurrection and Ascension (which are the revelation in successive phases of the one unchanging glory of God) His coming is a present fact; but our perception of His coming is something still growing as His Spirit guides us into all the truth, until at last we know even as we are known.

APPENDIX II

ON MORAL AND SPIRITUAL AUTHORITY

It may be objected that the Church should never in any circumstances employ force—at any rate, physical force. But I believe the objection is due, partly to a latent Manichæism which holds that matter is always evil, or at least "unspiritual," and partly to a very just fear that force may be wrongly used if its use is permitted at all. Yet there are some cases where the Church would plainly be not only at liberty, but morally bound, to use force.

Suppose a clergyman begins to give teaching that is absolutely at variance with the doctrine of the Church, the Church may appeal to his better feelings and ask him to resign; but if he will not, the Church must assuredly have the right to turn him out, and that, if necessary, by force.

No doubt in a civilised country what the Church does as a rule is to ask the State to act against the man, on the ground that he has broken contract and holds his position on false pretences. This is what the Mediæval Church called "handing the offender over to the secular arm."

But let us imagine the situation in a Mission Church where a convert has, for penance, been excluded from attendance at public worship for a period. Suppose he insists upon coming; then certainly the congregation would be right forcibly to remove him. Again, supposing the use of force as discipline may be of advantage to moral development (and up to a certain stage I am sure it may), and supposing there is no civilised State to employ it, the Church will be right to do what is best for the character of those for whom it is concerned. But no doubt all this is purely preparatory to the positive spiritual work of the Church, which must always take the form of appeal and not of force.

There is, however, so much confusion on the subject of moral and spiritual authority in general, that it may not be out of place to add here some remarks upon it.

The word "authority" is derived from a Latin word which may perhaps be best translated by "weight."

When we speak of a man of weight, or an opinion that carries weight, we have something very near the original meaning of the term authority. Sometimes we are inclined to think of authority as best represented by the political ruler, or the military commander. But these are not really typical kinds of authority. They are very special cases where authority is clothed with compelling force. But in the spheres of which we are thinking there is not necessarily present any compelling force at all. When we think of authority in religion, in its connection with morals and such questions, there is no force, at any rate necessarily, present at all, and the Church's authority in the true sense is not any the less because it does not practise the methods of the Inquisition: nor was it any greater in the days when to its own proper authority it added coercive power, appealing to people in the name of what is in itself not authority strictly speaking, at all. For if I believe just because the Church is an assembly of the saints of God and its formularies are summaries of their experience, then I am believing on the ground of the Church's authority. But if I believe because an officer of the Church threatens me with the rack in the case of disbelief, I am believing not because the Church has authority, but because I dislike physical pain.

So authority always in the end means weight—what carries weight with our judgment. We can weigh one authority against another; we may weigh the authority of one theologian with that of another by considering which has shown the greater knowledge of the subject in question and the sounder judgment in dealing with it. In moral questions we do as a matter of fact perpetually come back to the man of moral weight. And what constitutes his weight is to begin with a certain uprightness in his own character, and then a certain sympathy and insight which enables him to understand how he would apply to the circumstances of other people the principles by which he lives in his own. So, for example, Aristotle in the end determines all moral questions by reference to the standard which the man of moral sense would use; everything in the last resort is determined simply by his judgment. Virtue, he says, resides in a mean between two vicious extremes, and the mean is to be determined by a principle which the man of moral sense would use. Later on, after an interlude of two or three books wisely interpolated, he comes to ask, Who is the man of moral sense? and he turns out to be the man who has the right principle enabling him to determine the mean between vicious extremes; that is to say, that his standard of judgment in the end is simply the good, sensible man, and for practical purposes that does well enough, because for practical purposes we do know whose judgment we value, we do know who it is whose approval we should care to win, whose approval would of itself assure us that our conduct was right, and whose disapproval would of itself go far at least to assure us that our conduct was wrong, or at any rate that the matter needed careful reconsideration.

There is indeed another method than this of reliance upon the authority of a wise man, and it is represented by the other great thinker of Greece, by Plato. Plato's ideal method in moral questions was to try to determine the purpose of the whole universe and then determine how in any given circumstances a man may serve that purpose. The basis of his morals, in other words, was what we should call theological; and so far as we are able to apply this, it is the only finally satisfactory method; so far as we can say that the principles of Christianity imperatively demand some particular action or attitude of mind, we shall not care how little other authority we can quote, but shall say that we can see quite clearly that our allegiance to Christ and His religion involves a certain point of view for us; and if no one else has taken that point of view, provided we can find no flaw in our reasoning, we shall say none the less, This is the point of view which we, as Christians, are bound to take.

That has been the method by which, as a matter of fact, most Christian reforms have been carried out. That was the way by which, in an instance to which I shall return in a moment, slavery was abolished. Slavery had been tolerated by the Christian Church for centuries. The authority of the Christian Church might therefore have been quoted as substantially in favour of it. A very large number of Christians did, in fact, favour retaining it, because, of course, the abolition of the slave trade was an interference with property, and heartrending appeals were made in the name of "the unfortunate widow with a few strong blacks," as in our day appeals are made against legislation in the name of the widow who has shares in breweries. But Wilberforce's point of view was simply this, that whatever the Church may have said through all these centuries, when you look at the Christian principle of the right way to treat human beings it condemns slavery; and if all the Christians in all the ages had denied that, it would not have altered the fact that, as we see it—so Wilberforce and his friends would have urged—as we see it, slavery is condemned; that is enough for us; we go forward in the certainty that we are carrying out the will of God. Wilberforce brought people round to his point of view; now you will hardly find a Christian to defend slavery as an institution. Some day, perhaps, it will be the same with war.

But in most moral questions the authority to which we appeal is not that of the good and wise individual, but that of the moral sense of our civilisation. We can very seldom give an adequate reason for those points on which we have the strongest moral convictions. For example, in argument I suppose we should most of us find it very difficult to produce a case for monogamy as against polygamy anything like so strong as the feeling which we have in favour of the one against the other. That feeling is implanted in us by the experience of our civilisation, a civilisation which has, in fact, emerged from one into the other, and these very strong instinctive feelings, which are common to great masses of people and for which usually any one individual in all that mass can only give a most inadequate reason, are something to which an enormous volume of human experience has contributed. Generation after generation has come to feel that certain relations of the sexes are, as a matter of fact, the only ones that can be maintained with real wholesomeness, and this belief becomes so strong in the community that it is received with the air we breathe all through the formative years of our life, and the result is an intense conviction for which, as I say, we can hardly give any argument—an intense conviction that one sort of thing is right and the other wrong; and what most of us mean by our conscience is just this body of feeling concerning right and wrong which has been implanted in us as the result of the accumulated experience of civilisation. From the point of view of the individual it is usually more an emotion than a reasoned judgment; and it is much more of the nature of prejudice than of an argumentative conclusion. When people talk about conscientious objections to obeying the law, it is always quite impossible to distinguish between their prejudice and their conscience; there is no standard by which to determine. But the fact that it is unreasoned in the individual does not mean that it is irrational, or without reason in itself. What has been built up by the steady pressure of whole centuries of experience has enormous weight of pure reason behind it, even though the individual cannot himself give the reason, and even though there may be no individual alive who can give it; it has come out of the logic of experience; it has been built up in the strictly scientific way by a whole series of facts. There is an enormous inductive background, an enormous scientific basis for the moral convictions of the better, more self-controlled members of any civilised society. The moral verdict of society, and the conscience of the individual, which is his own echo, for the most part, of that moral verdict, is a thing of quite enormous authority.

But, it will be urged, the authorities clash. The verdict of European civilisation is for monogamy; the verdict of certain other civilisations is quite as emphatically against it. Does this mean that the whole distinction of right and wrong is a mere matter of convention? No, it does not. But even if it did, the thing would not be as bad as people often imagine, because convention is not something artificial in the sense of contrary to nature or fictitious; a convention is simply the expression of human nature working on a large scale. Man is a being whose nature it is to set up conventions, and a convention is a product of human nature, a property and mark of human nature, just as much gravitation is a property and mark of mechanical nature; and it only becomes contrary to nature and a nuisance when it has survived the purpose for which it originally grew up. But none the less there is something more than any convention or social growth about the distinction of right and wrong; the distinction in itself is absolute and fundamental. It is the distinction between recognising oneself as member of a community and not so recognising oneself. Morality is always recognition of a claim on the part of other persons, the recognition that their point of view and their interests have to be taken into account in the determination of my conduct. As man is by nature social, as by nature he is designed to live in communities, the distinction of right and wrong, that is the recognition of the claim of the community and of the members in it, is absolute and final.

But what is the content of the two terms right and wrong, what actual action shall be called right and what wrong on any given occasion, may vary easily according to circumstances, according to the degree of social development and the like. There is conduct which is right at one stage of society and wrong at another, precisely because at one stage it tends to the health of society, while at another it will be bad for the health of society; just as there are ways in which it is good from time to time to train children in which it would not be well to train grown-up people; and there is conduct which is appropriate to earlier stages of society, because beneficial to society, which becomes inappropriate and harmful at any other stage. What is right and what is wrong may depend very largely upon circumstances, stage of development, spiritual receptiveness, and a host of other things; but the distinction between right and wrong itself remains unaffected by all these, and absolutely fundamental and invariable.

Now, how is it that in society progress is actually made in morals? The appeal to authority can always be made in two ways. It can be made in the most obvious form in the interest of mere stagnation, by saying, "What was good enough for our fathers is good enough for us," a thing nobody ever does say; or by saying, "What is good enough for us is good enough for our children," a thing which numbers of people say. While the first form may be some safeguard against wild experiments—and wild experiments in morals are more dangerous than wild experiments anywhere else in life, for a reason I will mention in a moment—yet the tendency of this appeal is to pure stagnation. But the right appeal is to ask, not what the great men of the past actually did, but what were the principles upon which they acted. What we want to be doing with the prophets of the last generation is not saying again, like parrots, just what they said, but finding out the principles and spirit of their life and applying that same spirit to circumstances which are changed just because those prophets lived and wrought. They would not have been prophets, they would not have been great men, if they had not changed in some degree the world they lived in. Then just because they have changed the world their action may no longer be appropriate; it is not the action which they themselves would now take if they were still alive and retained their power of development. What we do then is to appeal, not to their conduct but to the principle of their conduct. So when Wilberforce started the campaign against slavery what he did was to appeal from the conduct of the Church to the principle of that conduct which it professed and admitted. In other spheres it admitted the sanctity of human personality; but it had never applied this principle to the particular problem of slavery.

In this way the appeal to authority is both just, safe, and progressive. It is only a fool who will throw away all that the experience of the ages has built up. But the wisest man of all is surely he who, rejoicing in that great inheritance, can still appeal not to its outward form, but to its indwelling, living spirit, and carry forward the work which the past has done. The ages in the past that we value are not those in which people were mainly concerned to praise their predecessors, but those in which men were agreed to press forward to whatever new life God has in store. So it must be here: if we would be true to the great men of the past, to the authority of those who have built up our moral life, it will not be by standing still, but by moving on in the direction to which they point.

The appeal to authority, then, will not be an appeal to practice, but always an appeal to principle; and so we shall be saved from that danger of moral experiment, a danger that is so immensely great because the individual who has made the experiment has thereby very often spoilt himself. One cannot experiment in the moral life with the detachment that we use in science. I may try mixing a couple of fluids together to see what happens, and I can regard the result quite accurately; but I cannot try the experiment of stealing, or of murder, in order to see what the real moral value of the thing is, because in the process of doing the act I shall vitiate my own soul; here the material in which we experiment is itself the instrument by which we have to judge; and the man who has once done an evil thing himself, very seldom has the same clearness of vision concerning its good and evil as the man who has kept true to some lofty purpose. The mere experiment, the mere trying what it feels like to be a murderer—not that anyone would take so extreme an instance as that—is always a method condemned in advance to futility, because in the process of making the experiment we destroy our power of judging the result. We want therefore to rely upon some authority; being unable to experiment for ourselves, we must follow the general rule that I have stated; the authority to which we appeal must be an authority of principle and not of practice.

But what of the authority of our Lord Himself? To us who have accepted it, or who are trying to accept it, it is final; yet still, surely, in the spirit rather than in the letter. Why did He teach by a series of amazing paradoxes if it was not to prevent us setting up a code of rules as His legislation, if it was not to force us back upon the spirit of His teaching, behind the detailed regulations in which that spirit was embodied? Even here it is still true that the appeal is to the authority of His Spirit and not to that of detailed action or individual precept.

And beyond all this, it is certain that He Himself wins His authority by first submitting Himself to the moral judgment of His people. He rejects, in the second and third of the Messianic temptations after His baptism, the method of coercion. He rejects this, and stands before men submitting Himself to their moral judgment, to their conscience, to their capacity to understand pure goodness and love, as that capacity has grown through the civilisation which God Himself had guided as the preparation for His final revelation in His Son. So He submits Himself first of all to our moral judgment; and thus our conscience, coming down to us, as it does, out of the Divinely-guided history of the past, is the supreme authority; if we choose Him to be the Guide of our life it is because our conscience has first pronounced Him to be the highest and the holiest, which we must needs love when we see it.

APPENDIX III

ON JUSTICE AND EDUCATION

As long as there are great numbers of citizens whose faculties are undeveloped it is impossible for society to be justly ordered. The democracies of the world have been curiously blind to this truth, as they have to the parallel truth that education is essential to true liberty.

As long as there is a vast difference between a man's actual worth to society and his potential worth, there will be two just claims concerning him, and no possibility of adjudicating between them. To treat a man who is in fact useless as though he were useful, is to injure the community by encouraging a parasite; to treat him as useless, when only lack of opportunity has prevented his becoming useful, is to injure him. A vast amount of the existing social order is an attempt to compromise between these two injuries, by inflicting a little of both. The only real solution is to be found in a complete educational system which will raise the actual worth of every man to the level of his potential work precisely by enabling him to realise his potentialities.

But education which is to have this effect, without producing mere selfishness and aggressiveness and thereby defeating its own object, must be a moralising force; and that means, if the argument of Appendix II is sound, that its processes must be largely sub-conscious. In fact, one root of the great sin of Germany is to be found in the effort to control life through the highly developed conscious intellect. The specialised training of administrators and the attempt to guide human action by scientific method is doomed to failure. If it were possible to collect all the relevant facts, it might be right merely to form an inductive conclusion and act upon it. But in regard of any human problem it is never possible to collect all the facts; they are at once too numerous and too subtly differentiated. Consequently the English method, though grotesquely deficient just where the German is strong, is yet morally preferable and politically more successful. It takes a boy and throws him into a society of boys which largely governs itself; appalling risks are taken and disasters are not unknown; boy standards are allowed to prevail, with the result that form-work is regarded as a tiresome though inevitable adjunct rather than the chief business of school life. Perhaps it is as well to mention here that the exaltation of games over work, however disastrous in its exaggeration, is yet morally sound; for the boy feels that in his games he plays for his house and school, while his work is done for himself. Wise seniors will tell him from the pulpit that he should work hard at school so as to fit himself for the service of the community in later years; and this is true enough; but the boy will be a terrible prig if he is continually conscious of its truth.

The same principle determines our University ideal. The primary test for a degree is "residence"—that is, an adequate share in a general life. Colleges may require attendance at lectures, but the University does not. It demands that a candidate for a degree should have some knowledge—not very much, it is true—but it never asks where or how he got it; it only asks if he has "kept his terms."

At the end of the process there are some failures, of course; but those who represent the system's success, and they are the great majority, though they may not have any large amount of knowledge, have acquired the instinct to act wisely in almost any emergency with which they may be confronted. Very often they could not give any theoretical ground for acting as they do, for their wisdom is largely sub-conscious or instinctive; but the action is right all the same.

In England we are at the present time witnessing the collision of two educational types, of which I have outlined the older and more traditional. But this collision is itself of such exceeding interest that, at the risk of some repetition, I would venture to sketch out the two opposing types and attempt to indicate the mode of their interaction.

The aim of education may be defined as the attempt to train men and women to understand the world they live in, so that they may be able to assist or resist the tendencies of their time in the light of ideals and standards resting on the widest possible foundation of knowledge and experience.

Now, our educational history for the last hundred years has been the result of the interaction between two predominant educational types, which I may call, simply for the purposes of description, the traditional and the modern. The traditional type comes down to us (with modifications, no doubt) by a continuous history from the Middle Ages, and its chief representatives in England at the present time are those large private institutions which are called public schools, and the two older universities. The first great mark of this type of education is that in practice—whatever its theory may have been—in practice it is corporate. It has believed in educating people rather through influence than through instruction, and it has believed in educating them in direct relation to their social context and setting. Now that, in a country of aristocratic organisation, inevitably involved an exclusive and aristocratic type of education. If you have got a society stratified in layers one above the other, and you are then going to educate people in direct relation to their social context, your educational system is bound to be similarly stratified. That is inevitable, and consequently, through the social conditions of the time, the education which is most strongly corporate in tone and spirit has also tended to be aristocratic. As I have said, this method deals with people rather through influence than through instruction. Of course, it does not ignore instruction, but it is true that not very long ago I heard a very distinguished lady asked whether a certain school was what we call a public school; "Oh, yes," she replied, "it is a real public school. I mean they don't learn anything there." The instruments which for the most part this education has used have been the great literatures of all ages, and particularly the literatures of Greece and Rome, and their civilisations. These literatures and civilisations have a great advantage over all others as instruments of education, because, while they are in many ways closely akin to our own, which are descended from them, they are complete and can be studied in their entirety. The aim of this type of education has been to bring the student's mind into closest possible contact with the greatest minds of the human race in all ages, with the minds that have done or attempted most (in history), with the minds that have thought most accurately and deeply (in science and philosophy), with the minds that have felt most tenderly and truly (in poetry). It may, or may not, succeed in that aim. It may attempt it in the case of individual students who are particularly ill-suited for it; but that is its aim, and no one is going to say that it is an ignoble aim. In doing this, it has supplied to those who have been most able to profit by it standards of judgment, standards of criticism. This enables a man to stand apart from the tendencies of the moment and to pronounce judgment on them in the light of what has been best in human experience. Those are the strongest points, as I consider, of the old traditional type. But it has certain faults, one of which I have already mentioned, which is a fault in our day if it was not a fault in the day in which this type of education became predominant. I mean that it is liable to be exclusive, to shut up people within the limits of their own class so that they are unable to acquire any living acquaintance with the great movements going on in the world around them.

The other system has not these particular evils; this more modern type of education, so far as you can draw lines across history at all, may be said to begin with Rousseau; it is predominantly individual rather than corporate, intellectual rather than spiritual, democratic rather than aristocratic; it supplies people with knowledge of facts rather than with standards of judgment. It is individual rather than corporate, for it began to take possession of the world when the forces of progress were almost all of them strongly individualistic; at that time the demand of democracy was for the abolition of privileges, the breaking down of class restrictions and the insistence that the individual must be able to live his own life; with all of which we entirely agree, though we think it needs a good deal of supplementing; and, consequently, its tendency has been to suggest to people that the aim of education is that they may get on in the world. The instrument which it has used has been for the most part instruction, and its appeal has been, not as in the traditional system to sympathy and imagination, but to intelligence and memory. This, it seems to me, is precisely because it believes in the career open to talent, and so far cuts across all social divisions.

Its ideal is the educational ladder. Now there would be no objection to the educational ladder if people went down it as well as up, if, that is to say, men of small ability and character always sank in the social scale and men of great ability and character always rose. But so long as you have social classes maintained in their position, not by ability and character alone, but by the mere accident of possession, so long it will be true that to lift a man by education from one social stratum to another is to expose him to a terrible temptation—the temptation to despise his own people. And when once a man's native sympathies have been rooted up, it is hard for any more to grow. There is real danger that the more modern type of education may serve to produce a race of self-seekers. But this modern type has great advantages. It is alive and in touch with the world at the moment; and the people who receive education of this kind will probably be very vitally aware of most of the living interests of their own time. But it fails to supply standards of judgment.

Now, of course, no existing institution belongs purely and entirely to either of these types; but we can all think easily of institutions in which one or the other is the predominant characteristic. And one of our troubles is that most parents like the faults and dislike the virtues of both types. They like the aristocratic and exclusive tone of the traditional type; and they like the pushfulness and "get-on-in-the-world" tone of the modern type.

The great problem before the educational world in the next period is to draw the two types and tendencies in education closer together, to leave the whole strength of both unimpaired, but to unite them. It is not easy to do. It is a very big problem, easily stated, but very hard to solve in practice. I would suggest that one of the flaws of the modern tendency is that it leaves people very strongly aware of what is going on at the moment, but not always equally aware of what has been thought by the greatest men in the history of the world. This is very liable to lead people to suppose that whatever is modern is on that account good. Now that is exactly as foolish as to suppose that whatever is ancient is therefore good. The fact its antiquity or modernity has nothing to do with its value at the present moment. Of course, it is true that any institution which has lasted through many centuries is likely to be of use again, though we may always have just reached the point at which it begins to be an incubus. Of course, it is true that an idea which arises out of the stress of life at the moment is very likely to be very well adapted to the realities of that moment in which it arises, but, also, it may be well adapted to assist a downward course. What we want is that the people shall know the facts and also have the power to judge them—to be able, as I said, to assist or resist the tendencies of their time, in the light of the best ideals and standards. There is a very strong inclination among many of us (I am personally very much aware of it in myself) to think that the new thing must be good; and yet one remembers the words of Clough:—

Again, the old type which trains people through their social setting is very largely co-operative in its methods. It merges the individual in his school, or his college, so that he comes quite genuinely to care more keenly for the welfare of his house and school and college than for his own progress. Nobody who has had any intercourse at all with the life of public schools or universities can doubt that. The modern method, on the whole, I suppose, trusts mainly rather to competition. It aims at assisting people to put out their best energy by pitting them against one another. I want to raise a very serious question to which I am not prepared to give an answer. I want all people interested in education to consider it. Is it worth while to get the greatest effort out of a person at the cost of teaching him that he is to make efforts in his own interest? I am very doubtful.

I heard a little while ago a distinguished schoolmaster describe the visit of the father of one of the boys in his house; the boy was being very idle, and this distinguished man said, "I wish you would speak to him as seriously as ever you can"; the father said, "I will." He saw the boy and when he came back he said, "I spoke to him very seriously, in fact I spoke to him quite religiously. I said 'You must be getting along, you know, or other people will be pushing past you.'" The religion would appeal to be of a "Darwinian" type.

Now I wish to express a purely personal conviction with regard to these two types of teaching, and it is this: while we have got to incorporate all, or at any rate, nearly all, that the more modern type of education has given us, it has got to be used in such a way as to leave the great marks of the traditional type predominant. Education, I hold, should remain primarily corporate rather than individual, primarily spiritual (that is, effective through influence, and through an appeal to sympathy and imagination), rather than primarily intellectual (that is, effective through an appeal to intelligence and memory), primarily concerned with giving people the power to pronounce judgment on any facts with which they may come in contact rather than supplying them simply with the facts. It should be primarily co-operative and not primarily competitive.

It is mainly the new democratic movements in education which have emphasised this view. Indeed, the Workers' Educational Association has understood more definitely than any other body I am aware of, that what it finds of supreme value in the great centres of education is the spirit of the place rather than the instruction; and those of us who have received the best, or at all events have been in a position to receive the best, that Oxford can give, and those who have had just a taste of her treasures at the Summer School, will agree that Oxford does more for us than any lectures do. But while we say that, we need also to insist on a greater energy and efficiency, a greater and more living contact with the world of to-day in some, at least, of the centres of the old traditional type. Yet it is the traditional type that must control, because the traditional type on the whole stands for spirit against machinery. I have no doubt it is true that the old schools and universities are amateurish in method; and I have no doubt that we ought to organise ourselves more efficiently. There is a good deal of waste that may be saved; but I shall regret the day when we become efficient at the cost of our spirit.

I believe that in the University Tutorial Classes organised by the Workers' Educational Association you will find upon the whole the soundest educational principles which are at this moment operative anywhere in England. The classes choose their own subjects, and, as a general rule, they choose those subjects about which nobody knows the truth. Those are always the best instruments of education; for if anyone knows the truth, he has only to say what it is and his hearers believe him. That may be instruction, but it is not education. Real education is always best conducted as a joint search for truth; and in these Tutorial Classes we have, not one teacher and thirty hearers, but thirty-one fellow students, one of whom has commenced the study earlier than the rest, and can therefore act as guide.

These are wide-reaching problems; and, indeed, there is no limit to the range of the influence of education. It is the supreme regenerative force. What is the chief obstacle of all who work for progress in any department of life? Always the apathy of those whom we especially wish to help. And why are they apathetic? Simply because they have had no opportunity of finding out what is the life from which they are excluded. But open by the merest chink the door of that treasure-house wherein are contained the garnered stores of literature and science, of history and art, and they will be foremost in demanding that they shall no longer be excluded from the birthright of the sons of civilisation. These are the good things of which no one is deprived because another possesses them; they are the true social goods of which possession by one redounds to the enrichment of all. It is the taste of them that can most stimulate the zeal for progress; and as it supplies the motive power, so it supplies also the directive wisdom. The perfecting and expansion of our education is just what is most vital for social progress to-day, and for the establishment of real justice in our social life, for it alone can bring within the reach of all that knowledge which is at once the source of power and the guarantee that the power shall be beneficent.

APPENDIX IV
ON ORDERS AND CATHOLICITY

The position taken in the text of these lectures might be summarised as follows: It is the living body which gives authority to its Orders; it is not the possession of valid Orders which gives authority to the body. In support of this view I have the kind permission of Dr. Headlam to quote the following from his article—"Notes on Reunion: The Kikuyu Conference," in the Church Quarterly Review for January, 1914.

"On December 20th, 1912, the Bishop of Madras delivered an informal speech to the members of the National Conference of Missionaries, at Calcutta. This created in India and elsewhere a considerable amount of sensation. As in that speech he referred to something which the present writer had written and to an article in the Church Quarterly Review by Dr. Frere,[#] and as his speech has been very widely misunderstood, I think I may be allowed to refer briefly to the points he raised. The views which he propounded were those which I had put forward in the 'Prayer Book Dictionary,' and I should like to be allowed to quote them again:

[#] "The Reorganisation of Worship," by W. H. Frere, D.D., Superior of the Community of the Resurrection, Mirfield (Church Quarterly Review, October, 1912).

"If we combine the Patristic theory of Orders with the rule of ordination, we shall be able to put the idea of Apostolic Succession into its right place. It is really a deduction from the right theory of Orders, and the mistake has been to make Orders depend upon Apostolic Succession and transmission.

"The authority to consecrate and ordain, or to perform all spiritual offices, resides in and comes from the Church to which God gives His Holy Spirit. From the beginning this work of the Church has been exercised by those who have received a commission for it, and the rule of the Church has been that that commission should always be given by those who have received authority from others with a similar commission. The historical fact, therefore, of Apostolic Succession has resulted from the rule of the Church being always regularly carried out. If this be correct, the following further deductions may be made:

"1. The idea of 'transmission' is an additional and late conception which, instead of expressing the idea of Succession, has, by its exaggeration of it led to a rigid and mechanical theory of the Ministry.

"2. As the grace of Orders depends upon the authority of the Church and not upon mechanical transmission, all objections from supposed irregularities of ordination are beside the point, and the opinions of churchmen and others who have maintained that in certain circumstances a presbyter may ordain are explained. Ordination depends upon the authority of the Church, and not the Church upon ordination.

"3. The idea of Succession, which results from the Church's rule of ordination, is an historical fact, and not a doctrine. It represents an external connection with the first beginnings of Christianity of infinite value for the Church; and nothing should be done to break such a connection, as it acts like a link for binding together the Churches as parts of a living whole.

"4. One part of the work of Christian reunion should be to restore and secure the links of Succession throughout the whole Christian world; but no rigidity or mechanical theory of Orders need compel us to deny divine grace to those separated from us.[#]

[#] The Prayer Book Dictionary (Sir Isaac Pitman and Sons, Ltd., 1912), p. 42.

"The particular point that I wish to emphasise is that there are two things to be separated—the one the rule of the Church, the other the theory of that rule. I do not believe that it would be possible on any Catholic principle to depart from the rule of the Church with regard to Orders; I should go further and say that I believe that no real reunion would ultimately be possible except on the basis of that rule. At the present time, however, continuous emphasis is laid on the theory of Orders, and that theory is often put as an extreme form of a mechanical conception of the Apostolic Succession. Now it is quite true that from the beginning Bishops have been looked upon as 'the successors' of the Apostles, but I can find no authoritative interpretation of that phrase other than that they perform at the present day those functions of the Apostles which were not miraculous or extraordinary.[#] Neither the formularies of the Church of England nor, so far as I am aware, those of any other Church, lay down any theory of ministry, and to impose, therefore, any such theory on the Church is to depart from Catholic tradition.

[#] See, for example, Van Espen, i. 16, 1. Council of Trent, Sessio xxiii., Cap. iv.

"An incidental result of this is that our attitude towards Sacraments of Nonconformist bodies will not partake of that rigid character which is so characteristic of some in the present day. We are glad to see that Dr. Sanday takes exception to these. 'It seems to me to be a very delicate matter, and, indeed, scarcely admissible for one Christian body to take upon itself to pronounce upon the validity or otherwise of the ministrations of another. I think that at least the question ought not to be put in that bald and sweeping form.' It is interesting to note that Dr. Pusey would have been equally averse to such language. He of course accepts the doctrine of Apostolic Succession in very definite form, but he writes as follows:

"'But while maintaining that they only are commissioned to administer the Sacraments who have received that commission from those appointed in succession to bestow it, we have never denied that God may make His own sacraments efficacious even when irregularly administered; we should trust it might be so.'

"It would be of great advantage if we were to speak of non-episcopal orders and sacraments as 'irregular,' which we know they are, not as 'invalid,' about which we know nothing."

With these words of Dr. Headlam I am in profound agreement. But there is another quite different matter to which I would allude. If the Church is indeed to be the vehicle of the power of Christ in its plenitude, it must be Catholic not only in principle and right, but in actual fact. Deeper than all divisions of "Catholic" and "Protestant" is the division of the great human family—European, Indian, Chinese, and so forth. These great civilisations must each bring its own gift, consecrated by the Spirit of Christ, to the life of the whole Body before that Body reveals the measure of the fulness of the stature of Christ. A merely European Church cannot be fully Catholic, nor can it ever do, even for Europe, what the Catholic Church is called by God to do for the nations which become its provinces.

APPENDIX V

ON PROVIDENCE IN HISTORY

The most outstanding facts in the history known to us, which plainly reveal the providential guidance of its course, are the careers of Alexander the Great and Napoleon. There had developed in Greece the whole spirit of civilisation in reference to the small problems of the city-state; the whole principle of civilisation which had been thus worked out was now established; Greek civilisation was so perfectly developed that it had even a perfect theory of itself in Plato and Aristotle. Just at this moment there appears upon the scene the absolutely amazing figure— Alexander of Macedon, himself the pupil of the man in whom the Greek spirit reached its final formulation. He carries that spirit in his astounding triumphs through Asia Minor and Syria to the Western Provinces of India. As a military achievement the mere leading of his troops to the banks of the Indus is one of the supreme wonders of the world. No doubt he was conscious of a mission to spread the gifts which Greece held in trust for humanity; but also no doubt he was very much concerned with the political fabric which his conquests set up. The moment his work is finished, he himself dies. Politically his Empire was not established and it immediately fell to pieces. Spiritually it remained. It supplied the inspiration of Chandra gupta, and the career of Asoka is unintelligible apart from Alexander. The arrival of the Greeks in India is, I am assured, the beginning of all that we now understand by Indian art. Far more important to the history of the world was the bringing of Greek culture into Palestine; this culture in itself was no doubt decadent, and the Chasidim and Pharisees were right enough to resist it: yet the leaven of this humanising influence is an essential part of the preparation for the Incarnation in the soil of Judaism. It is to be noticed that Galilee was a region particularly affected by the Greek influence and the settlement of Decapolis was still mainly Greek in the Gospel period. Asoka and St. Paul are not at all the kind of successors that Alexander would have anticipated or desired, but his conscious desires were utilised by Providence to serve an end of which he never dreamed. His early death before his Empire could be consolidated in a political sense is as markedly providential as his emergence at the precise moment of history when he appears upon the scene.

The case is similar with Napoleon. Alexander at his death was 32 years old. Napoleon was 52. He also appears at a critical moment, is active precisely as long as he can serve what we now see to have been the cause of progress, and is then removed. The great feature of the period is the growth of the sentiment of nationality. This is the sense of membership in a people united by common characteristics and a common purpose; it is therefore always democratic in spirit though it need not at all necessarily be democratic in machinery. The old European constitutions, which had been valuable enough in their time, were becoming a barrier to its further development; the flood of progress burst the dam in France, and soon after there appears the supreme genius, not himself a Frenchman, who was to carry the spirit of which France had just become consciously possessed through the entire length and breadth of Europe. Napoleon, like Alexander, was conscious of his mission; he thought of himself as being the organ of the Revolution; he is reported to have said that moral principles did not apply to him; they applied only to persons, and he was a force. But there can be no doubt that he was as much concerned with establishing a vast French Empire as he was with merely carrying the principles of the French Revolution into the other nations. He is allowed success so long as the work of destruction is still needed; his activities first as general and then as ruler began the unification alike of Italy and Germany; but as soon as the spiritual work which he was to do is fully accomplished, the political construction, which was as a great scaffolding surrounding it, falls to pieces, and he is driven into exile to end his days in solitude and impotence. Perhaps some day people will look back upon the horror that now lies upon the world and not only believe that God was active in it, but see the blessings which He was conferring by its means.

PRINTED IN GREAT BRITAIN BY

RICHARD CLAY AND SONS, LIMITED,

BRUNSWICK STREET, STAMFORD STREET, S.E.

AND BUNGAY, SUFFOLK.

* * * * * * * *

By the Rev. WILLIAM TEMPLE.

THE FAITH AND MODERN THOUGHT. SIX LECTURES. With an Introduction by Professor Michael Sadler.

THE KINGDOM OF GOD. A COURSE OF FOUR LECTURES.

THE NATURE OF PERSONALITY. A COURSE OF LECTURES.

STUDIES IN THE SPIRIT AND TRUTH OF CHRISTIANITY. BEING UNIVERSITY AND SCHOOL SERMONS.

REPTON SCHOOL SERMONS. STUDIES IN THE RELIGION OF THE INCARNATION.

FOUNDATIONS. A STATEMENT OF CHRISTIAN BELIEF IN TERMS OF MODERN THOUGHT. By Seven Oxford Men: B. H. STREETER, R. BROOK, W. H. MOBERLY, R. G. PARSONS, A. E. J. RAWLINSON, N. S. TALBOT, W. TEMPLE.

LONDON: MACMILLAN & CO., LTD.

14819636R00040

ISBN 9781530384082

9 781530 384082